Living the Restored Life

Richard T. Case
& Lawrence A. Collett

Copyright © 2015 by Richard T. Case & Lawrence A. Collett

All rights reserved. No portion of this book may be reproduced, stored in a retrieval system, or transmitted in any form or by any means © electronic, mechanical, photocopy, recording, scanning, or other © except for brief quotations in critical reviews or articles, without the prior written permission of the publisher.

Scripture taken from the NEW AMERICAN STANDARD BIBLE®
Copyright © 1960,1962,1963,1968,1971,1972,1973,1975,1977,1995 by The Lockman Foundation. Used by permission.

Published in Boise, Idaho by Elevate Faith, a division of Elevate Publishing.
www.elevatepub.com

For information please email: info@elevatepub.com.

ISBN (print): 978-1937498665
Printed in the United States of America

TABLE OF CONTENTS

ACKNOWLEDGEMENTS vii

PREFACE ix

INTRODUCTION xi

CHAPTER 1
EXPERIENCING A RESTORED LIFE 1
- Being "in Christ"
- The Result

CHAPTER 2
ABIDING IN CHRIST 15
- Principles
- The Process
- Keys
- The Outcome
- Bearing "Fruit"

CHAPTER 3
THE STEPS OF ABIDING: Hearing 33
- God's Voice
- What He Has to Say
- He is Ready to Communicate
- Other Voices
    - The World
    - False Teachers
    - The Evil One
    - Self
- Seek Clarification
- Stay "Camped Out"
- Avoid Acting Compulsively

CHAPTER 4
THE STEPS OF ABIDING: Spend Time in the Written Word . . . 55

CHAPTER 5
THE STEPS OF ABIDING: Prayer 73
- What Is Prayer?
- Hindrances to Effective Prayer
- Conditions to Answered Prayer
- Examples of Prayer

CHAPTER 6
THE STEPS OF ABIDING: Journaling 97

CHAPTER 7
THE STEPS OF ABIDING: Responding to the Father 107
- Surrender of Will
- Hear His Instruction and Guidance
- Respond with Obedience
- Remember to Record
- Schedule His Directed Activity

CHAPTER 8
CONCLUSION 119

DEDICATION

We wish to dedicate this book to our wonderful wives, Sherry Collett (married 50 years) and Linda Case (married 45 years). Together, we have experienced the truths in this book. We are truly thankful for the privilege of walking together in oneness with our spouses, who daily demonstrate what it means to walk with God in the Restored Life. As a result, our lives are blessed. Their encouragement and inspiration have provided the time and perseverance to finish these books and teach the material to others. They truly have been our partners in this endeavor.

ACKNOWLEDGEMENTS

This book started as a suggestion by Larry to Rich. At the time, Rich and Linda were hosting a series of overseas couples' retreats. The retreats provided time for worship, Bible study (led by Rich), and sightseeing. After six or seven of these, and with the domestic seminars that were also held at their retreat center or other facilities, it was observed that a significant amount of the material presented was related and connected to a much bigger story. The suggestion was to begin to consolidate and combine this material into a single text that would illustrate and narrate this story.

At that same time, Rich and Linda were not only leading a ministry, but also assisting churches in an interim advisory or pastoral capacity. In addition, they were running a family business, which needed constant attention and direction. Thus, while acknowledging the need to proceed with such a project, the time was just not available to move forward. Therefore, Larry started assembling the material and began to develop a rough outline of the book. Subsequently, Rich took the outline and put together an initial foundation of how the material should be connected and presented. At this time, it was predominantly a study guide. Later, the material was supplemented with more descriptive and explanatory commentary to expand the study into a book and reference text as well. Some of this was derived from Larry's unpublished study entitled "Kingdom Restoration."

With the counsel of Anna McHargue and Emily Sarver of Elevate Publishing, the original text was divided into two books. We are grateful for this insight as it provided the opportunity to delve more deeply into the subject matter without regard to length. *Living the Restored Life* is the second book from the original text.

We have added incidents that describe true experiences of living a restored life. While some will discount these as isolated experiences, this could not be farther from the truth. A restored, Kingdom life produces supernatural activity with frequency. Some is invisible to the human eye, but very real and present to the heart. Other activity is not only visible, but beyond human explanation. When one abides with the Father, it is reasonable to see Him in action.

Our thanks to numerous parties for their assistance and support in getting this project completed. We are deeply grateful to the many individuals and couples whose lives are a testimony to the veracity and applicability of the material in this book. This includes not only the various attendees of the seminars taught by Rich, but also those being mentored by both Rich and Larry through the CEO Forum. In addition, those individuals who continue to learn from their teaching provide a growing laboratory of real lives changed and enhanced by intentional movement to an abiding, Kingdom-driven relationship with the Father. A special note of appreciation to our wives for their assistance in editing and clarifying some of the material.

PREFACE

This book is the second of two books dealing with life: what one should expect from it and how it is to be lived. It is written from the perspective of a biblical life view. You will see scripture cited throughout. That is because the Bible is really about life: yours, ours, everyone's. The first book, *The Restored Life*, describes the awesome life Christ provided through His work on the cross, and His subsequent rule in the Kingdom of God. This sequel describes how we can actually live that life to the fullest during our time on earth.

Our objective in the first book was to move the reader to an awareness of what life can really be, now. It provides an understanding and description of the restoration provided by Christ and His rule since. It also emphasizes and demonstrates the reality of a restored life in our current position. We need not wait for some future date or event. This book is about living the life described in *The Restored Life*. As we desire to receive the blessings and benefits of the life Christ brought forth, we need to learn how to live that life; day by day and moment by moment. This is the objective of *Living the Restored Life*. We desire to focus on the process and provide the reader a framework for experiencing the reality of such a life. By doing so, we want the reader to deepen and enhance his eternity experience during this rare and unique time when two realms of reality are available.

At the center of living a restored life is the process of "abiding in Christ". This is the way we stay "in Christ", in the Spirit, in the Kingdom and in the presence of God. Through an abiding relationship we communicate, listen and respond to the Father. As we abide in Christ, the resources of the Kingdom, needed to complete the work given by the Father, are available for our lives. We experience "fruit" and see the spiritual activity of the Father at work.

Therefore, it is important to understand how we can truly abide in Christ and allow the restored life to become a reality. *Living the Restored Life* provides the insight, guidance and approach to help us activate this process in our lives.

Because of the importance of abiding to living this life, each individual component is covered in detail. We want this book not only to provide instruction into the process, but also to serve as a reference in guiding us to a deeper relationship with the Father. It helps to remember that living a restored life does not occur overnight. We must learn and practice abiding. We also need to "disconnect" from some of the methods, systems and learned behavior of our past. This usually can't happen immediately. Remember, our role is to stay connected to Christ. That's it! The more we try to intellectualize, supplement or enlarge this requirement, the less effective we will be. It is God who is doing the work. He allows us to participate and watch the results appear in our lives.

Abiding in Christ produces changed lives. It emits His image, character and activity. This is our expectation for the readers of this book.

INTRODUCTION

If we knew there was one step we could take that would drastically change our lives for the better, would we take it? Especially if it required us to change the way we make decisions and prioritize our activities. And what if the benefits were promises and blessings not yet experienced, even less visible?

The apostle Paul was writing to Timothy, whom he revered as his own son. Clearly he was a mentor to Timothy. He writes in II Timothy 6: 12 "Fight the good fight of faith. Take hold of the eternal life to which you have been called and about which you made the good confession in the presence of many witnesses". Paul knew Timothy understood what life was about and had even verbalized his belief in Christ and the life He provided (the restored life). Now it was time to live that reality. By all appearances, Timothy forged ahead and accepted Paul's exhortation.

Jesus defines the exceptional restored Kingdom life as worthy of investing all one has in its acquisition. In Matthew 13: 45 He compares the Kingdom to a fine pearl, so valuable that one should invest all his assets to obtain. In the prior verse, He uses the analogy of a treasure hidden in a field to describe this life. Again, He states it is worthy of disposing all one's wealth in order to obtain.

What are we willing to invest in a restored life? Jesus describes this, in John 10:10, to "live life to the full". In our first book, "The Restored Life", we closely studied that life and found it to be far greater and desirable than we could ever imagine. So our next challenge was to move forward and "take hold" of that life, the same one given to Timothy. We (believers at this time) are recipients of a unique opportunity to simultaneously experience two realms of reality. These are the physical reality of this world and its dimensions and the spiritual reality of God's Kingdom. God asks us to dwell in one (the physical) but to "be alive" in the other. That is why scripture tells us to consider ourselves strangers, sojourners and aliens in this world because we have our citizenship in the Kingdom.

Accepting Christ is the pre-requisite to entering the Kingdom. We must believe He is God's instrument to save us from the "Fall" and be restored to life. There is no other way. We must have Christ to have life (I John 5:12). We assume most of the readers of this book have already made that decision. If not, one should stop, right now, and consider whether or not to move forward. Living a restored life is impossible without Christ. We urge you to make that decision and move forward to claim what Christ has provided.

Experiencing the restored life is intended to be a normal part of everyday living. Therefore, to enjoy this abundant life, we are called to be full time Kingdom residents.

We know our willingness and ability to dwell in the Kingdom tends to be difficult since we still have "roots" in the world. Our desire is to live as the "new man" (person), to sever those worldly roots and be transformed into the nature of our Lord who gives us the power to live in the Kingdom.

So, let's get started on our quest to receive and experience the fullness of a restored life. Let's explore how that is accomplished and the choices and steps we can make for it become our reality. Let's begin to celebrate the victory Christ has won and allow it to be the foundation of the way we live.

CHAPTER I

Experiencing the Restored Life

Here is a question to ponder. How many Bible teachers and preachers have personally experienced what they are teaching? For that matter, how many of us have seen our biblical knowledge and theology demonstrated in our daily lives? In the book of James (1:22-25), the writer exhorts us to have our knowledge and understanding applied to everyday activities.

> *But prove yourselves doers of the word, and not merely hearers who delude themselves. For if anyone is a hearer of the word and not a doer, he is like a man who looks at his natural face in a mirror; for once he has looked at himself and gone away, he has immediately forgotten what kind of person he was. But one who looks intently at the perfect law, the law of liberty, and abides by it, not having become a forgetful hearer but an effectual doer, this man will be blessed in what he does.*

God created us to have a vibrant, loving relationship with Him. This relationship is eternal and after accepting Christ as Savior, we are at the beginning stage. This relationship can continue to deepen, mature and grow during our time on Earth as we move into closer contact with the Father. This restorative process brings the benefits and promises God designed us to receive in this life.

Therefore, we desire our knowledge to move us further into this reality. How does this happen? How do we personally witness and testify to our daily relational experience of the Father's work in our lives? This chapter is about the foundational need to be "in Christ" at all times. We will see what this means and how God's Kingdom becomes accessible. Chapter 2 discusses the step-by-step process of "abiding in Christ". Abiding is the way we stay "in Christ". The rest of the chapters explore the components of an abiding relationship with the Father and how they can become an integral part of our daily experience.

BEING "IN CHRIST".

Throughout the New Testament we see the phrase "in Christ". Being "in Christ", or "in Him", is essential and foremost to walking in the Spirit and living a restored life in the Kingdom of God. "It is the very root and essence of the new life of the Christian" (Lawrence Richards, *The Teacher's Commentary*, p.816).

Let's examine what scripture says about a true believer's position in Christ, the conditions necessary to remaining in Christ and receiving the benefits derived from being in that relationship.

It is the way we experience Christ.

ROMANS 6:4-11:

> *Therefore we have been buried with Him through baptism into death, so that as Christ was raised from the dead through the glory of the Father, so we too might walk in newness of life. For if we have become united with Him in the likeness of His death, certainly we shall also be in the likeness of His resurrection, knowing this, that our old self was crucified with Him, in order that our body of sin might be done away with, so that we would no longer be slaves to sin; for he who has died is freed from sin. Now if we have died with Christ, we believe that we shall also*

live with Him, knowing that Christ, having been raised from the dead, is never to die again; death no longer is master over Him. For the death that He died, He died to sin, once for all, but the life that He lives, He lives to God. Even so consider yourselves to be dead to sin, but alive to God in Christ Jesus.

We receive God through the presence of Christ in us and His work on the Cross. We (believers) are "in Christ" because we have been raised to a new life with Him. We are now free from sin, no longer captured by its false claims. As we live in Him, we are able to receive and experience the promised, abundant life.

It is our reconciliation with the Father.

ROMANS 14:7-9; 2 CORINTHIANS 5:15-20:

For not one of us lives for himself, and not one dies for himself; for if we live, we live for the Lord, or if we die, we die for the Lord; therefore whether we live or die, we are the Lord's. For to this end Christ died and lived again, that He might be Lord both of the dead and of the living…

…and He died for all, so that they who live might no longer live for themselves, but for Him who died and rose again on their behalf. Therefore from now on we recognize no one according to the flesh; even though we have known Christ according to the flesh, yet now we know Him in this way no longer. Therefore if anyone is in Christ, he is a new creature; the old things passed away; behold, new things have come. Now all these things are from God, who reconciled us to Himself through Christ and gave us the ministry of reconciliation, namely, that God was in Christ reconciling the world to Himself, not counting their trespasses against them, and He has committed to us the word of reconciliation. Therefore, we are ambassadors for Christ, as though God were making an appeal through us; we beg you on behalf of Christ, be reconciled to God.

Living "in Christ" requires the complete surrender and identification of our lives with Him. We no longer are to live in "self", but rather are connected to the life of Christ. When we are "in Christ", we actually become a different person. This is the process of transformation. Our old nature (the flesh, the self) is being transformed into Christ's nature. As this happens, we are reconciled and again united with the Father. We can then offer His reconciliation to others. We are equipped to be His representative, fulfilling His greater purposes in our lives and in the world.

It is the way we receive our inheritance.

EPHESIANS 1:9-14:

> *He made known to us the mystery of His will, according to His kind intention which He purposed in Him with a view to an administration suitable to the fullness of the times, that is, the summing up of all things in Christ, things in the heavens and things on the earth. In Him also we have obtained an inheritance, having been predestined according to His purpose who works all things after the counsel of His will, to the end that we who were the first to hope in Christ would be to the praise of His glory. In Him, you also, after listening to the message of truth, the gospel of your salvation—having also believed, you were sealed in Him with the Holy Spirit of promise, who is given as a pledge of our inheritance, with a view to the redemption of God's own possession, to the praise of His glory.*

When we are "in Christ", we "hear and believe" and have access to truth. We understand God has already designed His purposes (His predestined desires for each of us) for our lives. "In Christ", we join Him in this greater purpose.

THE RESULTS OF BEING "IN CHRIST" OR "IN HIM".

Outlined below are some of the specific attributes of living "In Christ". As you can see, the list is significant and includes many of the blessings, benefits and promises God intended for us. After perusing the list, spend time in the verses related to those desired attributes, allowing God to give them a deeper reality for your life.

1. **Abundant life**
   - Romans 6:1,11
   - I Corinthians 15:22
   - Ephesians 2:4,5
   - John 1:4

2. **The truth of eternity operates now**
   - Romans 6:23
   - John 3:15,16
   - John 4:14

3. **Freedom from guilt; not living in condemnation**
   - John 3:18
   - Romans 8:1
   - Ephesians 1:4

4. **Connecting to God's love, feeling and receiving His affection and pleasure**
   - Romans 8: 38,39
   - I John 2:5

5. **Possessing a passion for processing and enjoying truth**
   - Romans 9:1
   - Ephesians 4:21
   - I John 2:8

6. **Experiencing unity with other believers**
   - Romans 12:5
   - Galatians 3:28
   - Ephesians 2:21
   - Ephesians 3:6

7. **Being transformed (experiencing a changed life)**
   - I Corinthians 1:2

8. **Receiving and experiencing His grace (His favorable activity)**
   - I Corinthians 1:4
   - II Timothy 1:9

9. **Receiving and experiencing His wisdom**
   - I Corinthians 4:10
   - II Timothy 3:15 (of salvation)

10. **Receiving and experiencing God's promises**
    - II Corinthians 1:20

11. **Being fully committed to living in Christ**
    - I John 2:5,6

12. **Living in victory, not defeat**
    - II Corinthians 2:14

13. **Enjoying transparency with God**
    - II Corinthians 2:17
    - Ephesians 3:11,12

14. **Having a clear understanding of His will and desires**
    - II Corinthians 3:14
    - I John 1:5

15. **Experiencing a new creation, not hampered by the old nature, but being renewed**
    - II Corinthians 5:17

16. **Full reconciliation with God**
    - II Corinthians 5:19

17. **Living in full freedom**
    - Galatians 2:4

18. **Understanding I am fully justified**
    - Galatians 2:16

19. **Knowing I am a child of God**
    - Galatians 3:26

20. **Experiencing promises and blessings from God**
    - Ephesians 1:3
    - Ephesians 2:7

21. **Knowing and joining God's plan for good works**
    - Ephesians 2:10

22. **Experiencing and manifesting God's glory**
    - Ephesians 3:21
    - I Peter 5:10
    - II Thessalonians 1:12
    - Jeremiah 4:2

23. **Experiencing God's forgiveness**
    - Ephesians 4:32
    - Acts 10:43
    - Ephesians 1:7

24. **Experiencing joy**
    - I Peter 1:8
    - Psalm 66:6

25. **Experiencing and living out Christ's righteousness**
    - Philippians 3:9
    - II Corinthians 5:21
    - Psalm 92:15

26. **Receiving the "Prize"—the reward of being in His Kingdom**
    - Philippians 3:14

27. **Experiencing God's peace**
    - Philippians 4:7
    - Romans 15:13

28. **Having all my needs met**
    - Philippians 4:19

29. **Having fellowship with other believers**
    - Philippians 4:21

30. **Experiencing perfection (being made whole)**
    - Colossians 1:28
    - I John 3:5,6,9
    - II Samuel 22:31

31. **Receiving and experiencing the fullness of God**
    - Colossians 2:9,10

32. **Knowing I will receive a resurrected body**
    - I Thessalonians 4:16

33. **Having a heart of thankfulness**
    - I Thessalonians 5:18

34. **Experiencing salvation**
    - II Timothy 2:10

35. **Being able to appreciate and not feel burdened by adversity**
    - II Timothy 3:12
    - I Peter 3:16

36. **Experiencing answered prayer**
    - I Chronicles 5:20

37. **Experiencing and living in hope**
    - Job 13:15
    - Lamentations 3:25
    - Romans 15:12,13

38. **Experiencing God's protection**
    - Psalm 18:30
    - Proverbs 30:5
    - Psalm 37:40
    - Psalm 34:8,22
    - Psalm 64:10
    - Nahum 1:7

39. **Having a deep level of trust in God**
    - Psalm 28:7
    - Psalm 37:5
    - Daniel 3:28
    - Jeremiah 17:7

40. **Living with confidence that God has great and good plans**
    - Jeremiah 29:11-13
    - I John 5:14

41. **Experiencing the Holy Spirit**
    - John 7:39
    - Ephesians 1:13
    - Ephesians 2:22
    - I John 3:24
    - I John 4:13

42. **Bearing Kingdom "fruit"**
    - John 15: 5

43. **Not living in shame or disappointment**
    - Romans 9:33

- Romans 10:11
- I Peter 2:6
- I John 2:28

44. **Having the knowledge, understanding and ability to speak God's Word**
    - I Corinthians 1:5
    - I John 5:20

45. **Having a firm foundation in life**
    - II Corinthians 1:19
    - Colossians 1:17
    - Ephesians 2:7

46. **Experiencing redemption**
    - Ephesians 1:7

47. **Receiving an inheritance**
    - Ephesians 1:11

48. **Being anointed**
    - I John 2:27

49. **Experiencing purity**
    - I John 3:3

SUMMARY

Being "in Christ" summarizes the way we experience the fullness of the restored life. As can be seen from the comprehensive list of results, our lives become like Christ. We become a part of Him and we begin to reflect His image rather than our own. All this not only benefits us, but can also be passed to others. Clearly, in order to be "in Christ", we need to become attached to Him and He needs to reside in us. Being "in Christ" is the realization of being "born again". It happens when we make that critical decision to accept Him and when we decide, daily, to live in His presence.

We now face another question. How do we live "in Him" after we have made that decision? The rest of this book helps us answer that question. We want reality, not just theology. We want living "in Christ" to be a daily experience rather than a lofty goal that seems to be beyond our grasp.

REFLECTION

How do we view our lives? Do we see them as driven by our own knowledge and intellect or as contained within the will and direction of Christ? Chances are we all are trying to live within our own recognizance, seeking help from prayer only when needed. However, we now grasp that living a life "in Christ" is much different. In the next chapters we will learn how to live and experience the life Christ has provided. What do we see in our lives that needs to be changed in order to begin this process?

_____

_____

_____

_____

_____

Experiencing the Restored Life

CHAPTER 2

What Is "Abiding" In Christ?

Being "in Christ" provides the ability to receive all the promises of God and to experience the reality of His Kingdom. It is only through Him we gain access to the King, His resources and His blessings. Christ has prepared the "way" and opened the entrance to the Kingdom. What a blessing and privilege to be able to follow our Savior into this eternal dwelling!

We need not worry *how* that happens, because Christ has already assured its reality. We do, however, have a choice to make. The choice is whether or not to stay "in Christ" or to follow our own instincts and intellectual persuasions. Assuming we elect to stay in Christ, what must we do to allow ourselves to be transformed and become the persons God created us to be?

The answer lies in the "abiding" process. As we will see in John 15, the only way our lives can be of any value or create any benefit is to abide in Christ and to stay connected to Him. In this chapter we will take a closer look at abiding: what it is, how is works, and what emerges from the process.

DEFINITION

To abide means to dwell, remain, stay and live in. As we have learned, living in the Kingdom means we are living "in Christ". In order to be living "in Christ", it is essential that we abide. Otherwise, we miss experiencing the Kingdom of God.

JOHN 15:5

> "*I am the vine, you are the branches; he who abides in Me and I in him, he bears much fruit,* **for apart from Me you can do nothing***.*"

PARTICIPANTS IN ABIDING

JOHN 15:1-5

> "*I am the true vine, and My Father is the vinedresser. Every branch in Me that does not bear fruit, He takes away; and every branch that bears fruit, He prunes it so that it may bear more fruit. You are already clean because of the word which I have spoken to you. Abide in Me, and I in you. As the branch cannot bear fruit of itself unless it abides in the vine, so neither can you unless you abide in Me. I am the vine, you are the branches; he who abides in Me and I in him, he bears much fruit, for apart from Me you can do nothing.*"

In this passage we are able to identify the different parts of the Vineyard, the outcome of abiding in the Vine and the nature of our responsibility.

1. **The Vine (v.1)** – Christ is the Vine, the source of all life. He is the foundation supporting the wisdom, truth, resources and life of the Kingdom.

2. **The Vinedresser (v.1)** – God is the keeper of the vineyard. He directs the Vine and all the aspects of the plant.

3. **The Branch (v.4)** – We, as believers, are the branches. Our charge is to stay attached to the Vine. We do not produce anything, but rather "bear" the fruit that comes forth. Apart from the Vine, nothing is accomplished.

What Is "Abiding" In Christ?

4. **The Result (v.4-5)** – The ultimate result is the production of fruit and more fruit. It is a continuous process that improves with time. Fruit is the activity of the Father in our lives, benefiting others as well as ourselves.

5. **The Choice (v.4)** – Our choice is to remain and abide in the Vine. We need to stay "in Christ". That's it! By remaining there, we will watch fruit produced. If we choose to leave, we are useless.

KEY PRINCIPLES IN ABIDING
JOHN 8:28-32,36

> *So Jesus said, "When you lift up the Son of Man, then you will know that I am He, and I do nothing on My own initiative, but I speak these things as the Father taught Me. And He who sent Me is with Me; He has not left Me alone, for I always do the things that are pleasing to Him." As He spoke these things, many came to believe in Him. So Jesus was saying to those Jews who had believed Him, "If you continue in My word, then you are truly disciples of Mine; and you will know the truth, and the truth will make you free." They answered Him, "We are Abraham's descendants and have never yet been enslaved to anyone; how is it that You say, 'You will become free?'" Jesus answered them, "Truly, truly, I say to you, everyone who commits sin is the slave of sin. The slave does not remain in the house forever; the son does remain forever. So if the Son makes you free, you will be free indeed."*

1. Jesus and the Father are fully united in their work. Jesus only does what the Father wants Him to do.

2. Staying "in Christ" and dwelling on what He says are the key elements of discipleship.

3. Truth is a by-product of being a disciple of Christ.

4. Freedom is found only by remaining "in Christ".

Doing what pleases the Father and listening to Him are important. Abiding leads to truth; truth takes us to freedom. We are to develop a passion for abiding and for truth. We need to stay in the Word and intimacy with the Father. We then experience the promised freedom and transformation.

THE PROCESS OF ABIDING

Jesus' Provision

JOHN 14:12-18, 23-27

> "*Truly, truly, I say to you, he who believes in Me, the works that I do, he will do also; and greater works than these he will do; because I go to the Father. Whatever you ask in My name, that will I do, so that the Father may be glorified in the Son. If you ask Me anything in My name, I will do it. If you love Me, you will keep My commandments. I will ask the Father, and He will give you another Helper, that He may be with you forever: that is the Spirit of truth, whom the world cannot receive, because it does not see Him or know Him, but you know Him because He abides with you and will be in you. I will not leave you as orphans; I will come to you…*"

> Jesus answered and said to him, "*If anyone loves Me, he will keep My word; and My Father will love him, and We will come to him and make Our abode with him. He who does not love Me does not keep My words; and the word which you hear is not Mine, but the Father's who sent Me. These things I have spoken to you while abiding with you. But the Helper, the Holy Spirit, whom the Father will send in My name, He will teach you all things, and bring to your remembrance all that I said to you. Peace I leave with you; My peace I give to you; not as the world gives do I give to you. Do not let your heart be troubled, nor let it be fearful.*"

What Is "Abiding" In Christ?

Notice the provision we have been given to allow us to be "in Christ" and abide with Him. Also notice the absence of rules and regulations. The Father has provided Himself to assure us of the ability to have such a relationship.

We are not alone. We have a Father who loves and cares for us. The Spirit dwells in us and can communicate to us. The whole Trinity resides in us. This is why we experience the fullness of God. The result is "divine peace". We can live in complete peace, regardless of circumstances.

The Role of the Holy Spirit

JOHN 16:12-16; ROMANS 8:26-28

> *"I have many more things to say to you, but you cannot bear them now. But when He, the Spirit of truth, comes, He will guide you into all the truth; for He will not speak on His own initiative, but whatever He hears, He will speak; and He will disclose to you what is to come. He will glorify Me, for He will take of Mine and will disclose it to you. All things that the Father has are Mine; therefore I said that He takes of Mine and will disclose it to you...."*
>
> *In the same way the Spirit also helps our weakness; for we do not know how to pray as we should, but the Spirit Himself intercedes for us with groanings too deep for words; and He who searches the hearts knows what the mind of the Spirit is, because He intercedes for the saints according to the will of God. And we know that God causes all things to work together for good to those who love God, to those who are called according to His purpose.*

These verses describe the role of the Holy Spirit in the abiding process. He guides us and relates what the Father tells Him. He speaks truth and transfers it from Christ to us. The Spirit tells what is to come and intercedes according to the will of God (which means He communicates God's will on a daily basis). There is constant dialogue between the Spirit and the Father. The aim is to understand and reveal the will of God. While the process is beyond our ability to understand, it always works to our benefit. All things work for our good, even if we have strayed outside the Kingdom through our poor choices. God will redirect His efforts to move us toward His will.

Clearly hearing God's voice and understanding His will.

ISAIAH 30:15-23

> *For thus the Lord GOD, the Holy One of Israel, has said, "In repentance and rest you will be saved, In quietness and trust is your strength." But you were not willing, and you said, "No, for we will flee on horses," Therefore you shall flee! "And we will ride on swift horses," Therefore those who pursue you shall be swift. One thousand will flee at the threat of one man; you will flee at the threat of five, Until you are left as a flag on a mountain top And as a signal on a hill. Therefore the LORD longs to be gracious to you, and therefore He waits on high to have compassion on you. For the LORD is a God of justice; How blessed are all those who long for Him. O people in Zion, inhabitant in Jerusalem, you will weep no longer. He will surely be gracious to you at the sound of your cry; when He hears it, He will answer you. Although the Lord has given you bread of privation and water of oppression, He, your Teacher will no longer hide Himself, but your eyes will behold your Teacher. Your ears will hear a word behind you, "This is the way, walk in it," whenever you turn to the right or to the left. And you will defile your graven images overlaid with silver, and your molten images plated with gold. You will scatter them as an impure thing, and say to them, "Be gone!" Then He will give you rain for the seed which you will sow in the ground, and bread from the yield of the ground, and it will be rich and plenteous; on that day your livestock will graze in a roomy pasture. Also the oxen and the donkeys, which work the ground, will eat salted fodder, which has been winnowed with shovel and fork. On every lofty mountain and on every high hill there will be streams running with water on the day of*

What Is "Abiding" In Christ?

the great slaughter, when the towers fall. The light of the moon will be as the light of the sun, and the light of the sun will be seven times brighter, like the light of seven days, on the day the LORD binds up the fracture of His people and heals the bruise He has inflicted.

The Lord is waiting to bless us with compassion and grace. He waits for us to surrender and walk in the Spirit and in His Kingdom. We are to accept His will and passionately seek Him. The Lord usually wants to move incrementally (step by step), while we want to know the whole picture before we move. We will hear what God has to say from "behind", which means we will hear Him without necessarily being able to see the result in our vision or in our thinking. We must rely on His word rather than our own abilities and skills. Because of our limited senses, we are not always able to understand what He is doing. The Spirit gives direction to help us stay in the Father's will. Then as a result of hearing and following, we will discard things in our lives that are not aligned with His character or instruction. We can experience all the fullness of the promised, Covenant blessings.

KEYS TO ABIDING

Listen and obey God, letting Him direct your life.

Proverbs 3:1-6

My son, do not forget my teaching, But let your heart keep my commandments; for length of days and years of life and peace they will add to you. Do not let kindness and truth leave you; Bind them around your neck, Write them on the tablet of your heart. So you will find favor and good repute in their understanding. Trust in the LORD with all your heart and do not lean on your own understanding. In all your ways acknowledge Him, and He will make your paths straight.

In order to have God direct our steps, we need to abide. As we abide, we receive His instruction as truth that becomes central to what we think, say or do. This builds our trust in Him, diminishing our reliance on what we think is right. We learn to subordinate our will to His and follow as He directs.

Stay in the presence of the Lord.

Psalm 37:1-8

> *Do not fret because of evildoers, Be not envious toward wrongdoers. For they will wither quickly like the grass and fade like the green herb. Trust in the LORD and do good; Dwell in the land and cultivate faithfulness. Delight yourself in the LORD; And He will give you the desires of your heart. Commit your way to the LORD, Trust also in Him, and He will do it. He will bring forth your righteousness as the light and your judgment as the noonday. Rest in the LORD and wait patiently for Him; Do not fret because of him who prospers in his way, Because of the man who carries out wicked schemes. Cease from anger and forsake wrath; Do not fret; it leads only to evildoing.*

We must trust and abide in Him and in His Word. We need to be excited about following His way. We become still before Him and wait for guidance without fretting or worrying whether or not He will respond. Finally, we refrain from anger. He promises to provide what we truly need and is best for us. That is why it is so important to stay in the presence of the Lord.

Be open and available for pruning.

John 15:2

> *"Every branch in Me that does not bear fruit, He takes away; and every branch that bears fruit, He prunes it so that it may bear more fruit."*

What Is "Abiding" In Christ?

"Pruning" is a term that tends to cause fear and anxiety. It shouldn't! We can see from the above verse it is necessary and desirable to improve our abiding relationship. Pruning means cutting back the healthy parts of the branches. Without pruning, branches can continue to grow (sometimes in a disproportionate manner). If left alone, the sap will be insufficient to flow to the growing branch. If not pruned, the tree will not produce viable fruit and may provide no fruit whatsoever. Thus the Vinedresser prunes these branches so they remain healthy and the sap (the Holy Spirit) can flow into the fullness of the fruit.

Practically speaking, this means the Lord will cut back our activities and involvements because we are too busy and spread so thin. Pruning allows us to receive the fullness of His desires for our lives. He will cut back our activities so we live simpler lives and have rest, recreation and time to be refreshed. This enables the Holy Spirit to produce fruit, more fruit and much fruit. We may be proud of all our activities and think they are pleasing God. In fact, we can be so fully engaged in our own agenda and may actually produce nothing the Father desires. The Father prunes our lives so we bear His fruit and remain productive.

Let His words remain in you.

John 15:7-8

> *"If you abide in Me, and My words abide in you, ask whatever you wish, and it will be done for you. My Father is glorified by this, that you bear much fruit, and so prove to be My disciples."*

The word "Rhema" in Greek means God's specific application of His written word (*logos*) to our lives. Our role is to be in the written Word He is directly speaking. We are to stay in these words until they become truth for us. As this occurs, we understand what is on His heart and in His will. Then we can pray what He has spoken. He promises to fulfill what we pray. We will see His supernatural work occur in the very fabric of our lives.

Focus on hearing what He has to say.

LUKE 10:38-42

> *Now as they were traveling along, He entered a village; and a woman named Martha welcomed Him into her home. She had a sister called Mary, who was seated at the Lord's feet, listening to His word. But Martha was distracted with all her preparations; and she came up to Him and said, "Lord, do You not care that my sister has left me to do all the serving alone? Then tell her to help me." But the Lord answered and said to her, "Martha, Martha, you are worried and bothered about so many things, but only one thing is necessary, for Mary has chosen the good part, which shall not be taken away from her."*

There is a difference between working for God (serving Him with programs and activities) versus listening to Him. It is important that we stay in His presence and listen. Martha was so busy working for God and was not actually receiving anything from Him. Her mind was occupied by activities of service. The Greek derivative refers to a very selfish motive (to receive approval from the master). Mary, on the other hand, chose the better thing (abiding) by sitting at His feet and listening to what He had to say. This wasn't a sermon Mary was hearing, but back-and-forth dialogue. It helped her gain a better understanding of what Christ was saying. This example is critical because it teaches the importance of hearing and understanding what is on God's heart and knowing His will.

Heed the Father.

PROVERBS 4:1-10; 20-23

> *Hear, O sons, the instruction of a father, And give attention that you may gain understanding, for I give you sound teaching; Do not abandon my instruction. When I was a son to my father, Tender and the only son*

What Is "Abiding" In Christ?

in the sight of my mother, Then he taught me and said to me, "Let your heart hold fast my words; Keep my commandments and live; Acquire wisdom! Acquire understanding! Do not forget nor turn away from the words of my mouth. Do not forsake her, and she will guard you; Love her, and she will watch over you. The beginning of wisdom is: Acquire wisdom; and with all your acquiring, get understanding. Prize her, and she will exalt you; She will honor you if you embrace her. She will place on your head a garland of grace; She will present you with a crown of beauty. Hear, my son, and accept my sayings, And the years of your life will be many..."

My son, give attention to my words; Incline your ear to my sayings. Do not let them depart from your sight; Keep them in the midst of your heart. For they are life to those who find them and health to all their body. Watch over your heart with all diligence, for from it flow the springs of life."

We need to draw His Word from the pages of scripture into our innermost thoughts where it can become truth and operate in our everyday lives. We must pay attention and focus on what He says. It actually does little good to only complete a Bible study. Rather, we are to spend time where He is specifically speaking to us. As we pay attention and meditate on what He is saying, we should avoid setting it aside and pursuing other items. We must engraft His Word in our heart so it becomes real. We are to "guard" His words by not deviating from what He says. We can then acquire His understanding and allow Him to bring a sense of wholeness and freshness into our lives.

Stand firm and take the next step based upon what God has spoken to you.

I JOHN 2:24-27

As for you, let that abide in you, which you heard from the beginning. If what you heard from the beginning abides in you, you also will abide

> in the Son and in the Father. This is the promise, which He Himself made to us: eternal life. These things I have written to you concerning those who are trying to deceive you. As for you, the anointing which you received from Him abides in you, and you have no need for anyone to teach you; but as His anointing teaches you about all things, and is true and is not a lie, and just as it has taught you, you abide in Him.

We need to walk step by step with the Father. As we abide, we begin to receive clarity of His instruction. We then accept His word as truth and abide further as He reveals His next steps. There is no need for advisors as we rely on the Holy Spirit for specific guidance and instruction. This is significant! Abiding helps us understand what God wants us to do and accomplish. It begins the process of changing our character and transforming our entire being into His image.

Follow the Holy Spirit.

JOHN 14:16-26

> "I will ask the Father, and He will give you another Helper, that He may be with you forever; that is the Spirit of truth, whom the world cannot receive, because it does not see Him or know Him, but you know Him because He abides with you and will be in you. I will not leave you as orphans; I will come to you. After a little while the world will no longer see Me, but you will see Me; because I live, you will live also. In that day you will know that I am in My Father, and you in Me, and I in you. He who has My commandments and keeps them is the one who loves Me; and he who loves Me will be loved by My Father, and I will love him and will disclose Myself to him". Judas (not Iscariot) said to Him, "Lord, what then has happened that You are going to disclose Yourself to us and not to the world?" Jesus answered and said to him, "If anyone loves Me, he will keep My word; and My Father will love him, and We will come to him and make Our abode with him. He who does

What Is "Abiding" In Christ?

> *not love Me does not keep My words; and the word which you hear is not Mine, but the Father's who sent Me. These things I have spoken to you while abiding with you. But the Helper, the Holy Spirit, whom the Father will send in My name, He will teach you all things, and bring to your remembrance all that I said to you."*

Following the Holy Spirit requires us to transfer the leadership of our lives, so He can lead and guide us. The process is actually quite passive on our part. Our decision is to stay in an abiding relationship. If we do, the Spirit brings truth into our lives by speaking God's words to us. As we communicate with the Father through the Holy Spirit, our role is to dialogue, understand and receive further clarity. We then receive His guidance and the ability to recall His instruction. These instructions are always intended to keep us walking in the Kingdom of God, where we are protected and His promised blessings are made available.

THE OUTCOME OF ABIDING

Truth and Freedom

JOHN 8:28-36

> *So Jesus said, "When you lift up the Son of Man, then you will know that I am He, and I do nothing on My own initiative, but I speak these things as the Father taught Me. And He who sent Me is with Me; He has not left Me alone, for I always do the things that are pleasing to Him." As He spoke these things, many came to believe in Him. So Jesus was saying to those Jews who had believed Him, "If you continue in My word, then you are truly disciples of Mine; and you will know the truth, and the truth will make you free." They answered Him, "We are Abraham's descendants and have never yet been enslaved to anyone; how is it that You say, 'You will become free'?" Jesus answered them, "Truly, truly, I say to you, everyone who commits sin is the slave of sin. The slave*

> does not remain in the house forever; the son does remain forever. So if the Son makes you free, you will be free indeed."

Truth and freedom result from abiding. As we abide, we will know the truth in God's heart. The more we experience truth, the more it frees us from pursuing other areas where it is not present. We will no longer be captured by the world's requirements or stipulations, but will be experiencing the beauty, joy and freedom of life lived in real, godly truth.

Our Desires Are Fulfilled

PSALM 37:3-5

> *Trust in the LORD and do good; Dwell in the land and cultivate faithfulness. Delight yourself in the LORD; And He will give you the desires of your heart. Commit your way to the LORD, Trust also in Him, and He will do it.*

As the Father's desires become established in our hearts, He wants us to abide so we can begin to discern how He wants to fulfill them. We are now free to express them to God and allow Him to reveal how and when He will fulfill them. The key is to allow our own selfish desires to be displaced by His will. Then we know we will receive what is best and will have a better experience of His presence and His Kingdom.

Answered Prayer

JOHN 15:7,8

> *"If you abide in Me, and My words abide in you, ask whatever you wish, and it will be done for you. My Father is glorified by this, that you bear much fruit, and so prove to be My disciples…"*

We receive answers to our prayers and there is evidence of God's leadership in our lives. As we abide we more fully understand God's will

What Is "Abiding" In Christ?

and thus will ask the Father to accomplish His work. He supernaturally manifests His miraculous power as we witness and experience answered prayer. We realize our lives are made for His purposes and reverently desire to follow Him in all things.

Alignment with the Lord

Luke 10:38-42

> *Now as they were traveling along, He entered a village; and a woman named Martha welcomed Him into her home. She had a sister called Mary, who was seated at the Lord's feet, listening to His word. But Martha was distracted with all her preparations; and she came up to Him and said, "Lord, do You not care that my sister has left me to do all the serving alone? Then tell her to help me." But the Lord answered and said to her, "Martha, Martha, you are worried and bothered about so many things; but only one thing is necessary, for Mary has chosen the good part, which shall not be taken away from her."*

There is security, assurance, and a sense of eternal significance in our lives. It will be a pleasure to sit securely at the feet of Jesus, understanding His eternal perspective and purposes, and enjoying sweet fellowship. We begin to grasp what is truly important as He expresses Himself to us personally.

Discernment

John 16:13-15

> *"But when He, the Spirit of truth, comes, He will guide you into all the truth; for He will not speak on His own initiative, but whatever He hears, He will speak; and He will disclose to you what is to come. He will glorify Me, for He will take of Mine and will disclose it to you. All things that the Father has are Mine; therefore I said that He takes of Mine and will disclose it to you."*

As we are abiding and receiving all the Holy Spirit provides, we will understand truth, have great discernment, grasp things to come and receive Christ's fullness into our life. Many think this is beyond the experience of Christians in this life. But God's written and spoken word tell otherwise. We clearly begin to grasp what life is about and the awesomeness of our God and Savior.

Fruit

GALATIANS 5:22, 23.

> *But the fruit of the Spirit is love, joy, peace, patience, kindness, goodness, faithfulness, gentleness, self-control; against such things there is no law.*

JOHN 15:7,8

> *"If you abide in Me, and My words abide in you, ask whatever you wish, and it will be done for you. My Father is glorified by this, that you bear much fruit, and so prove to be My disciples..."*

God's fruit is being produced in our life. It is His fruit, produced through abiding, and not created on our own (remember, we can do nothing apart from Christ). There are two fundamental types of fruit. First there is the transformation of our soul, and our sinful nature. His nature, reflecting the Fruits of the Spirit, gradually becomes our new nature. Then we see the fulfillment of His Will where God changes circumstances and performs supernatural works. Only He can do this!

SUMMARY

The basics of abiding are to stay connected, listen, be obedient and watch fruit grow. Sound like nuclear physics? I don't think so! But this is what the Father asks us to do.

When my son was a teenager, he and I went on a float trip with a friend and neighbor. He had never been in a canoe before and I had

What Is "Abiding" In Christ?

rather limited boating experience. But it seemed a good way to spend the day and to get some "quality time" together. As we stepped into the canoe, I moved toward one side and so did he. You can guess the result. It immediately tipped and all our food and clothing was now water-soaked. What a way to start! When I got back in the boat, I was grumpy and grouchy. I wanted to blame him, but I wasn't sure it was his fault. I had never given him any instructions about keeping balance in the canoe and was not paying much attention myself. I was generally disgusted with the whole picture and with what appeared ahead.

Interestingly, when we returned to the canoe and began to grasp how we could work together, we found the trip to be quite enjoyable. We tried to coordinate our oars and worked together to get through the rapid spots. We also started to dry off and the day turned out to be an enjoyable one. The key was to stay in the canoe! If we got out, it was not going to be a good time.

In that same way, we as abiding Christians need to stay connected and work together with the Father. He knows how to row our boat and we need to learn to stay with Him, depend on Him, listen to Him and do what He says. If we go out on our own, it can be a real mess! Leadership is really staying in the "leader's ship". We can learn and experience so much about life by doing so.

THOUGHTS

The abiding process is the key to staying "in Christ" and receiving the benefits of a restored life. We have been given the necessary resources, but must still make a decision to do so. That decision requires a willingness on our part to accept the reality of Christ living in us, and a desire to have His will and character reflected in all we do.

In what ways have you avoided or obstructed this decision? What will you now do to allow the process of abiding to become a reality in your life?

Living The Restored Life

CHAPTER 3

The Steps Of Abiding: Hearing His Voice

Suppose you were trying to build a relationship with someone else. You desire to spend time with that individual. However, when you do, the following sequence of events transpires. First, you say how important this person is to you. Then you explain all the problems and obstacles you are facing in your life and ask the other person to do something about them. Before the individual can respond, you describe issues in the lives of others and relate how you want them addressed. Finally, you emphasize how much you like being a friend and walk away before one word is even spoken in response. This happens every time you get together.

What kind of relationship would that be? Why would anyone bother to stay engaged in that type of communication? I seriously doubt we would continue if we were on the receiving end of the discussion. The truth is, this scenario is similar to our conversations with the Father. We unload everything on our agenda, add "in Jesus' name" and "Amen," and leave. While God wants us to "cast our burdens on Him," He really desires a deeper relationship beyond a one-way conversation.

Ponder the following three statements.

- *What do we have to tell God that He doesn't already know?*

- *What does He have to tell us that we don't already know?*
- *What, then, is the best use of our time together?*

Because He is omniscient, God already knows everything we have to say. And, because we are limited and He knows no boundaries, we know nothing about His revelation to us. Clearly, our time is best spent listening. However, we rarely do! As we shall see in this chapter, hearing God speak is crucial to an abiding relationship with Him.

WE MUST HEAR WHAT HE HAS TO SAY.

This was demonstrated by Jesus.

During His time on Earth, Jesus stated that hearing the Father's voice was how He lived, at all times and in all things.

JOHN 5:16-30

> *For this reason therefore the Jews were seeking all the more to kill Him, because He not only was breaking the Sabbath, but also was calling God His own Father, making Himself equal with God. Therefore Jesus answered and was saying to them, "Truly, truly, I say to you, the Son can do nothing of Himself, unless it is something He sees the Father doing; for whatever the Father does, these things the Son also does in like manner. For the Father loves the Son, and shows Him all things that He Himself is doing; and the Father will show Him greater works than these, so that you will marvel. For just as the Father raises the dead and gives them life, even so the Son also gives life to whom He wishes. For not even the Father judges anyone, but He has given all judgment to the Son, so that all will honor the Son even as they honor the Father. He who does not honor the Son does not honor the Father who sent Him. Truly, truly, I say to you, he who hears My word, and believes Him who sent Me, has eternal life, and does not come into judgment, but has passed out of death into life. Truly, truly, I say to you, an hour is coming and*

The Steps Of Abiding: Hearing His Voice

> *now is, when the dead will hear the voice of the Son of God, and those who hear will live. For just as the Father has life in Himself, even so He gave to the Son also to have life in Himself; and He gave Him authority to execute judgment, because He is the Son of Man. Do not marvel at this; for an hour is coming, in which all who are in the tombs will hear His voice, and will come forth; those who did the good deeds to a resurrection of life, those who committed the evil deeds to a resurrection of judgment. I can do nothing on My own initiative. As I hear, I judge; and My judgment is just, because I do not seek My own will, but the will of Him who sent Me."*

Clearly, Christ had a special relationship with the Father. Christ says He joined the work He saw the Father doing and went where the Father was working, based on what the Father was saying directly to Him. Christ did not decide for Himself, what to do every day. He only did what the Father told Him. He avoided participation in any activity that was not directed by the Father. If this is how Christ operated while on Earth, demonstrating how life is to be experienced with the Father, shouldn't we be including Him more often in our decisions?

God speaks constantly.

He is speaking to each of His children, every day.

JOHN 10:1-5; 25-30

> *"Truly, truly, I say to you, he who does not enter by the door into the fold of the sheep, but climbs up some other way, he is a thief and a robber. But he who enters by the door is a shepherd of the sheep. To him the doorkeeper opens, and the sheep hear his voice, and he calls his own sheep by name and leads them out. When he puts forth all his own, he goes ahead of them, and the sheep follow him because they know his voice. A stranger they simply will not follow, but will flee from him, because they do not know the voice of strangers..."*

Jesus answered them, "I told you, and you do not believe; the works that I do in My Father's name, these testify of Me. But you do not believe because you are not of My sheep. My sheep hear My voice, and I know them, and they follow Me; and I give eternal life to them, and they will never perish; and no one will snatch them out of My hand. My Father, who has given them to Me, is greater than all; and no one is able to snatch them out of the Father's hand. I and the Father are one."

Hebrews 3:1-7; 14-15; 4:7

Therefore, holy brethren, partakers of a heavenly calling, consider Jesus, the Apostle and High Priest of our confession; He was faithful to Him who appointed Him, as Moses also was in all His house. For He has been counted worthy of more glory than Moses, by just so much as the builder of the house has more honor than the house. For every house is built by someone, but the builder of all things is God. Now Moses was faithful in all His house as a servant, for a testimony of those things which were to be spoken later; but Christ was faithful as a Son over His house—whose house we are, if we hold fast our confidence and the boast of our hope firm until the end. Therefore, just as the Holy Spirit says, "Today if you hear his voice…"

For we have become partakers of Christ, if we hold fast the beginning of our assurance firm until the end, while it is said, "Today if you hear his voice…"

He again fixes a certain day, "Today," saying through David after so long a time just as has been said before, "Today if you hear his voice…"

I Corinthians 2:9-16

But just as it is written, "Things which eye has not seen and ear has not heard, and which have not entered the heart of man, all that God has prepared for those who love Him." For to us God revealed them through the Spirit; for the Spirit searches all things, even the depths of God. For who among men knows the thoughts of a man except the spirit of the man which is in him? Even so the thoughts of God no one knows except the Spirit of God. Now we have received, not the spirit of the world, but the Spirit who is from God, so that we may know the things freely given to us by God, which things we also speak, not in words taught by human wisdom, but in those taught by the Spirit, combining spiritual thoughts with spiritual words. But a natural man does not accept the things of the Spirit of God, for they are foolishness to him; and he cannot understand them, because they are spiritually appraised. But he who is spiritual appraises all things, yet He, himself, is appraised by no one. For who has known the mind of the Lord, that he will instruct Him? But we have the mind of Christ.

If we truly follow Christ, we will hear His voice. A shepherd does not speak periodically to his sheep. He is always speaking, now, today and every day. There is not a day that we cannot hear from the Father. Since Christ responded only to what the Father spoke, He was getting direction every day. He did not go through periods of silence. If we are experiencing silence from God it means we have stopped hearing, not that He has ceased speaking. He reveals what is on His heart and mind, not based on our intellects, analytical skills or physical sense of what we see and hear. Rather, His communication is a spiritual process as He speaks through the Holy Spirit in ways we can understand. Our role is to receive His revelation. Thus as we abide in the Word, we are to receive what He speaks. We are constantly to be in a receiving mode since He is the speaker and we are the hearers.

God invites His children to listen, hear and follow as He communicates His nature, heart, purposes, ways and specific will.

It involves spiritual sensitivity

Matthew 11:13-15

"For all the prophets and the Law prophesied until John. And if you are willing to accept it, John himself is Elijah who was to come. He who has ears to hear, let him hear."

It is characteristic of one belonging to God.

John 8:45-47

"But because I speak the truth, you do not believe Me. Which one of you convicts Me of sin? If I speak truth, why do you not believe Me? He who is of God hears the words of God; for this reason you do not hear them, because you are not of God."

"My sheep hear My voice, and I know them, and they follow Me…

It is a requirement to know truth.

John 18:33-37

*Therefore Pilate entered again into the Praetorium, and summoned Jesus and said to Him, "Are You the King of the Jews?" Jesus answered, "Are you saying this on your own initiative, or did others tell you about Me?" Pilate answered, "I am not a Jew, am I? Your own nation and the chief priests delivered You to me; what have You done?" Jesus answered, "My kingdom is not of this world. If My kingdom were of this world, then My servants would be fighting so that I would not be handed over to the Jews; but as it is, My kingdom is not of this realm." Therefore Pilate said to Him, "So You are a king?" Jesus answered, "You say correctly that I am a king. For this I have been born, and for this I have come into the world, to testify to the truth. **Everyone who is of the truth hears My voice."***

It leads to faith.

The Steps Of Abiding: Hearing His Voice

Romans 10:17

So faith comes from hearing, and hearing by the word of Christ.

We are to surrender our lives to the Father, having spiritual ears to hear, being motivated and expecting to hear His voice. As we hear, He calls us to respond in obedience, following the very instructions He speaks. This requires a tender heart and a desire to pursue and receive truth. Upon understanding the truth, we follow completely in simple obedience. This process leads to faith. We know from Hebrews 11:6 that without faith it is impossible to please God. It is critical to abide in the Word, hear His voice, and let faith be produced. We can live a life that fully pleases God.

GOD IS ALWAYS READY TO SPEAK AND COMMUNICATE WITH HIS CHILDREN AS THEY LIVE IN RELATIONSHIP WITH HIM.

Matthew 7:7,8

"Ask, and it will be given to you; seek, and you will find; knock, and it will be opened to you. For everyone who asks receives, and he who seeks finds, and to him who knocks it will be opened."

Acts 17:26-30

And He made from one man every nation of mankind to live on all the face of the earth, having determined their appointed times and the boundaries of their habitation, that they would seek God, if perhaps they might grope for Him and find Him, though He is not far from each one of us; for in Him we live and move and exist, as even some of your own poets have said, 'For we also are His children.' Being then the children of God, we ought not to think that the Divine Nature is like gold or silver or stone, an image formed by the art and thought of man. Therefore having overlooked the times of ignorance, God is now declaring to men that all people everywhere should repent...

REVELATION 3:20-22

"Behold, I stand at the door and knock; if anyone hears My voice and opens the door, I will come in to him and will dine with him, and he with Me. He who overcomes, I will grant to him to sit down with Me on My throne, as I also overcame and sat down with My Father on His throne. He who has an ear, let him hear what the Spirit says to the churches."

REVELATION 22:17

The Spirit and the bride say, "Come." And let the one who hears say, "Come." And let the one who is thirsty come; let the one who wishes take the water of life without cost.

God wants to dialogue with His children. He promises to respond to us, including opening and closing avenues to guide us into His will. This relationship serves as the very essence of our being. It enables us to relate to our Creator on a very personal level. He is constantly engaging our hearts. He desires to come into our hearts and fellowship together. He will dialogue, express His truth and respond to our questions. This allows us to overcome the very obstacles we face every day. The Father freely offers His living water (spiritual nourishment) and invites us to receive and enjoy this provision.

GOD'S VOICE IS REAL AND RELATIONAL.

Hearing His voice is not limited to a theological study of Scripture or a religious interpretation in broad, general terms. Rather, His voice is personal, relational, real, and transmitted in a way we can hear regardless of our maturity level. We can experience Him as a loving Father.

The Steps Of Abiding: Hearing His Voice

John 10:3-5,16,27

"To him the doorkeeper opens, and the sheep hear his voice, and he calls his own sheep by name and leads them out. When he puts forth all his own, he goes ahead of them, and the sheep follow him because they know his voice. A stranger they simply will not follow, but will flee from him, because they do not know the voice of strangers…"

"I have other sheep, which are not of this fold; I must bring them also, and they will hear My voice; and they will become one flock with one shepherd."

"My sheep hear My voice, and I know them, and they follow Me."

James 1:5-8

But if any of you lacks wisdom, let him ask of God, who gives to all generously and without reproach, and it will be given to him. But he must ask in faith without any doubting, for the one who doubts is like the surf of the sea, driven and tossed by the wind. For that man ought not to expect that he will receive anything from the Lord, being a double-minded man, unstable in all his ways.

Psalm 95:6-11

Come let us worship and bow down, Let us kneel before the LORD our Maker. For He is our God, and we are the people of His pasture and the sheep of His hand. Today, if you would hear His voice, Do not harden your hearts, as at Meribah, As in the day of Massah in the wilderness, "When your fathers tested Me, They tried Me, though they had seen My work. For forty years I loathed that generation, and said they are a people who err in their heart, And they do not know My ways. Therefore I swore in My anger, Truly they shall not enter into My rest."

Isaiah 30:18-26

> *Therefore the LORD longs to be gracious to you, and therefore He waits on high to have compassion on you. For the LORD is a God of justice; How blessed are all those who long for Him. O people in Zion, inhabitant in Jerusalem, you will weep no longer. He will surely be gracious to you at the sound of your cry; when He hears it, He will answer you. Although the Lord has given you bread of privation and water of oppression, He, your Teacher will no longer hide Himself, but your eyes will behold your Teacher. Your ears will hear a word behind you, "This is the way, walk in it," whenever you turn to the right or to the left. And you will defile your graven images overlaid with silver, and your molten images plated with gold. You will scatter them as an impure thing, and say to them, "Be gone!" Then He will give you rain for the seed which you will sow in the ground, and bread from the yield of the ground, and it will be rich and plenteous; on that day your livestock will graze in a roomy pasture. Also the oxen and the donkeys, which work the ground will eat salted fodder, which has been winnowed with shovel and fork. On every lofty mountain and on every high hill there will be streams running with water on the day of the great slaughter, when the towers fall. The light of the moon will be as the light of the sun, and the light of the sun will be seven times brighter, like the light of seven days, on the day the LORD binds up the fracture of His people and heals the bruise He has inflicted.*

As a child learns to hear, distinguish, and relate to his parent's voice, so we are with our Father's. He will speak personally to us. As we seek to hear His voice, He promises to communicate and speak with clarity about the very questions we ask Him. He asks us to have certainty we will hear His voice and not waiver. We may be confused about what He says because it may be beyond our immediate understanding or seem inconsistent with our prior history, experience or intellectual comprehension. In reverence and awe of God, we need to be in a process of constant dialogue with Him. We should seek to hear more of what He has to say. When we do, He promises to speak to us.

Again, this communication does not depend on our spiritual experience or maturity. He will speak to us in ways we can understand. The way we speak to a teenager is different than the way we speak to a toddler. We change our communicaiton so each can better understand. They then respond in their own manner. This is what God promises to do with us. We can be assured if we ask for wisdom, He will speak to us. He will be speaking every day, all the time. He asks us not to neglect His voice or to discard His message. This can happen when we struggle against the message or try to test Him. We do this by asking Him to do things we desperately want, but are unwilling to surrender our will to His. As we cry out to Him, seeking to hear His voice, He promises to respond and to direct our steps specifically, even providing the details (turning right or turning left). We can know which way to go because He desires to communicate His wonderful plan and to give us His blessed promise of abundant life.

OTHER VOICES ARE OUT THERE!

While living in the world, we encounter numerous voices that attempt to distract. Because the nature of the world is self-centered, the goal of the enemy is to convince us we actually cannot hear God's voice clearly. We then will be left to our own devices to determine our path. With our limited understanding, we invariably walk down the wrong one. Thus we need to understand how these different worldly voices operate and to only respond to the Father's voice.

The World's Voice

Isaiah 29:13-15

> *Then the Lord said, "Because this people draw near with their words and honor Me with their lip service, But they remove their hearts far from*

Me, And their reverence for Me consists of tradition learned by rote, Therefore behold, I will once again deal marvelously with this people, wondrously marvelous; And the wisdom of their wise men will perish, And the discernment of their discerning men will be concealed. Woe to those who deeply hide their plans from the LORD, and whose deeds are done in a dark place, And they say, 'Who sees us?' or 'Who knows us?'"

CORINTHIANS 1:18-25; 3:18-20

For the word of the cross is foolishness to those who are perishing, but to us who are being saved it is the power of God. For it is written, "I will destroy the wisdom of the wise, and the cleverness of the clever I will set aside." Where is the wise man? Where is the scribe? Where is the debater of this age? Has not God made foolish the wisdom of the world? For since in the wisdom of God the world through its wisdom did not come to know God, God was well pleased through the foolishness of the message preached to save those who believe. For indeed Jews ask for signs and Greeks search for wisdom; but we preach Christ crucified, to Jews a stumbling block and to Gentiles foolishness, but to those who are the called, both Jews and Greeks, Christ the power of God and the wisdom of God. Because the foolishness of God is wiser than men, and the weakness of God is stronger than men. Let no man deceive himself. If any man among you thinks that he is wise in this age, he must become foolish, so that he may become wise. For the wisdom of this world is foolishness before God. For it is written, "He is the one who catches the wise in their craftiness"; and again, "The Lord knows the reasonings of the wise, that they are useless."

The world's voice claims to promote Christ and Christianity, but in reality denies Him and His truth. It does this by making Him appear irrelevant and by promoting its own agenda. It rejects a commitment to follow Him and disclaims any real value in doing so. The world claims to hold all wisdom and encourages us to follow its systems and methods instead of God's wisdom. God's wisdom is made to seem foolish in light of the world's. As a result, we are encouraged to dismiss God's wisdom and pursue the world's, because it seems more "logical" and "normal". In reality it translates what is true and valuable into things that are false and useless. We accomplish very little while experiencing the delusions of the world.

The Voices of False Teachers

MATTHEW 5:18-19

> "For truly I say to you, until heaven and earth pass away, not the smallest letter or stroke shall pass from the Law until all is accomplished. Whoever then annuls one of the least of these commandments, and teaches others to do the same, shall be called least in the kingdom of heaven; but whoever keeps and teaches them, he shall be called great in the kingdom of heaven."

EPHESIANS 5:6-7

> Let no one deceive you with empty words, for because of these things the wrath of God comes upon the sons of disobedience. Therefore do not be partakers with them.

I TIMOTHY 6:3-5

> If anyone advocates a different doctrine and does not agree with sound words, those of our Lord Jesus Christ, and with the doctrine conforming to godliness, he is conceited and understands nothing; but he has a morbid interest in controversial questions and disputes about words, out of which arise envy, strife, abusive language, evil suspicions, and constant friction between men of depraved mind and deprived of the truth, who suppose that godliness is a means of gain.

II Timothy 4:3,4

For the time will come when they will not endure sound doctrine; but wanting to have their ears tickled, they will accumulate for themselves teachers in accordance to their own desires, and will turn away their ears from the truth and will turn aside to myths.

II Peter 2:1-5

But false prophets also arose among the people, just as there will also be false teachers among you, who will secretly introduce destructive heresies, even denying the Master who bought them, bringing swift destruction upon themselves. Many will follow their sensuality, and because of them the way of the truth will be maligned; and in their greed they will exploit you with false words; their judgment from long ago is not idle, and their destruction is not asleep. For if God did not spare angels when they sinned, but cast them into hell and committed them to pits of darkness, reserved for judgment; and did not spare the ancient world, but preserved Noah, a preacher of righteousness, with seven others, when He brought a flood upon the world of the ungodly

False prophets are just that – false. They pretend to teach truth, especially Christian truth, but in fact are operating in the world, outside the Kingdom. They are not teaching what is on the heart and mind of God, but instead are promoting false doctrines and answers. They actually teach disobedience to God. Their teaching is characterized by words that sound good but are empty of meaning or power. They also promote controversy, and friction, attempting to gather followers by suppressing or distorting truth. By doing so, they actually rob their followers of the truth. They are truly selfish, seeking their own personal agendas, and often aim to increase their number of followers and their financial support. As a result they introduce erroneous thinking, encourage shameful habits and bring the truth into question. If a believer is walking outside the Kingdom, he has no spiritual discernment, and will often fall for the attractiveness of false teaching. This is particularly dangerous when believers are not abiding, and do not use God's written Word as a standard of truth.

The Voice of the Evil One

MATTHEW 13:37-39

> *And He said, "The one who sows the good seed is the Son of Man, and the field is the world; and as for the good seed, these are the sons of the kingdom; and the tares are the sons of the evil one; and the enemy who sowed them is the devil."*

JOHN 8:42-44

> *Jesus said to them, "If God were your Father, you would love Me, for I proceeded forth and have come from God, for I have not even come on My own initiative, but He sent Me. Why do you not understand what I am saying? It is because you cannot hear My word. You are of your father the devil, and you want to do the desires of your father. He was a murderer from the beginning, and does not stand in the truth because there is no truth in him. Whenever he speaks a lie, he speaks from his own nature, for he is a liar and the father of lies."*

EPHESIANS 2:1-3

> *And you were dead in your trespasses and sins, in which you formerly walked according to the course of this world, according to the prince of the power of the air, of the spirit that is now working in the sons of disobedience. Among them we too all formerly lived in the lusts of our flesh, indulging the desires of the flesh and of the mind, and were by nature children of wrath, even as the rest*

The Evil One speaks in a variety of ways. His objectives are to kill, steal and destroy. He is relentless, and works overtime to prevent believers from abiding, walking in the Kingdom and thus receiving power against him. His approach is to use temptation to draw people out of the Kingdom and then prevent them from going back. Whenever the Word is planted in a person's heart (usually through church preaching, reading scripture, devotions or listening to a sermon), the Evil One sows deception and untruth to crowd out and diminish the impact of the Word. He is a liar and the originator of lies, and he promotes disobedient thoughts as well as thoughts against God. The Evil One uses difficult circumstances to create discouragement and resignation, leading people to the false notion that pursuing God is not attractive because of painful experiences in their lives. He knows that an abiding believer, walking in the Kingdom and in the Spirit, is protected. The Father has already defeated him through Jesus. There is no ability to overcome God's will. Only when we walk outside the Kingdom does the Evil One have an influence to keep believers from knowing and experiencing God's will.

The Voice of "Self"

In addition to the voices of the world, of false teachers and of the Evil One, we also will experience the desires of our own earthly flesh (self). It is usually driven by our personal desires and intellect. When the voice of the Father speaks of things that counter those desires, our internal desires can begin to oppose what we have heard, because we can be self-centered and pursue our desires rather than His will.

PROVERBS 28:26

He who trusts in his own heart is a fool, but he who walks wisely will be delivered.

PROVERBS 19:21

Many plans are in a man's heart, but the counsel of the Lord will stand.

James 4:13-17

Come now, you who say, "Today or tomorrow we will go to such and such a city, and spend a year there and engage in business and make a profit." Yet you do not what your life will be like tomorrow. You are just a vapor that appears for a little while and then vanishes away. Instead, you ought to say, "If the Lord wills, we will live and also do this or that. But as it is, you boast in your arrogance; all such boasting is evil. Therefore, to one who knows the right thing to do and does not do it, to him it is sin.

James 4:1-3

What is the source of quarrels and conflicts among you? Is not the source your pleasures that wage war in your members? You lust and do not have; so you commit murder. You are envious and cannot obtain; so you fight and quarrel. You do not have because you do not ask. You ask and do not receive, because you ask with wrong motives, so that you may spend it on your pleasures.

I Corinthians 2:4-5

...And my message and my preaching were not in persuasive words of wisdom, but in demonstration of the Spirit and of power, so that your faith would not rest on the wisdom of men, but on the power of God

Our natural tendency is to make all our own decisions, big and little. Certainly, God wants us to make decisions. The issue is how we make them. We become used to making them on a daily basis. If we are only trusting in our own logic, we can have problems. When we are dependent on our own thinking, we only have our own knowledge, experience and perspective to serve as the basis for our conclusions. Such thinking can be futile and unproductive if it leaves God out of the equation. God wants us to use the minds He has given us, but to make all of our thoughts "captive" to His will. We are to pass our ideas and conclusions through Him. He alone possesses the wisdom and knowledge to give us the right direction.

DON'T ACT COMPULSIVELY ON EMOTIONS OR CIRCUMSTANCES.

I Samuel 10:7-8

"It shall be when these signs come to you, do for yourself what the occasion requires, for God is with you. And you shall go down before me to Gilgal; and behold, I will come down to you to offer burnt offerings and sacrifice peace offerings. You shall wait seven days until I come to you and show you what you should do."

I Samuel 13:8-14

Now he waited seven days, according to the appointed time set by Samuel, but Samuel did not come to Gilgal; and the people were scattering from him. So Saul said, "Bring to me the burnt offering and the peace offerings." And he offered the burnt offering. As soon as he finished offering the burnt offering, behold, Samuel came; and Saul went out to meet him and to greet him. But Samuel said, "What have you done?" And Saul said, "Because I saw that the people were scattering from me, and that you did not come within the appointed days, and that the Philistines were assembling at Michmash, therefore I said, 'Now the Philistines will come down against me at Gilgal, and I have not asked the favor of the Lord.' So I forced myself and offered the burnt offering." Samuel said to Saul, "You have acted foolishly; you have not kept the commandment of the Lord your God, which He commanded you, for now the Lord would have established your kingdom over Israel forever. But now your kingdom shall not endure. The Lord has sought out for Himself a man after His own heart, and the Lord has appointed him as ruler over His people, because you have not kept what the Lord commanded you."

Our normal reaction is to act when nothing seems to be happening or if obstacles begin to arise. That is what Saul did, and the consequences were enormous. God is always trying to get our attention. He is trying to speak to our hearts. Quite often, we are moved by a thought or idea and begin to suspect we should be taking action. We direct our time and activity accordingly. This can lead down a destructive path unless we first try to clarify the thought or idea through the Father. Sometimes we think the Father has spoken but can understand little or only a small part of His message. We tend to think, believe, sense or feel that we should respond in a certain manner. At this point, these are emotional responses and may or may not be appropriate. When we think, feel, sense or believe we should do something, God is really telling us to come closer to hear directly what He is saying. He will clarify the message so we can then act with confidence.

Circumstances may lead us to conclude we should take a certain action. Again, we should not respond solely to these circumstances. They should actually drive us to the Father so He can clarify what He desires to happen. Generally, circumstances will confirm what the Father has already revealed. They should never be used as a substitute for hearing from Him.

We need to remember our thinking may not be aligned with the Fathers if we are not in an abiding relationship. Partial, incomplete and unspoken thoughts need to have confirmation. Otherwise, we are probably acting from a motive that may not be in concert with the Father's will.

SUMMARY

The ability to "hear" from God is clear in scripture. In reality God is always speaking. He speaks through His written and spoken Word.

The two will never contradict each other. He also speaks through the Church. He can use circumstances to validate and support His pronouncements.

Many believers have erroneously stated, "God told me." And those errors have embarrassed both them and the Church. Many have used that statement to justify what they desire rather than God's will. These kinds of occasions, combined with the lack of hearing God's voice in their own lives, lead many to conclude they cannot hear the Father speak. As a result, this critical component of abiding is missing in their life experience.

This highlights the importance of really knowing when the Father is speaking. At its foundation is a need for surrender and transparency before the Father. Receiving direction from other sources can be dangerous and misleading. Using the Father to justify our own desires is a form of false teaching that carries huge negative consequences. One never should substitute their "glory" for that of the Father's. That happens when His voice is used to justify actions He has not authorized, supported or initiated.

Hearing the Father is an important part of the abiding relationship. Remember how often we need to listen to a voice before we begin to discern and recognize it immediately. It may take some time, but eventually we get to the point where we can distinguish that voice from the thousands of others heard on a daily basis. That is why Jesus said, "My sheep hear My voice. The sheep follow him, the shepherd, for they know his voice". (John 10). We must cultivate the practice of listening and hearing as we seek to abide with the Father.

A REAL TESTIMONY

A couple that had little Bible knowledge attended one of our week-long retreats in Europe. They were so excited about learning to abide and hear God's voice that they went home to the church and openly shared this excitement. Several men, who were leaders in the church, asked if the husband could teach them how to hear God's voice. He said he was just learning all this, but he knew a person, Rich, who could teach them. So we began a weekly conference call with the only requirement to have a heart to hear and to abide in the Word. They were thinking that would take months, if not years, of spiritual growth to be able to hear God's voice, but it was not the case. What they experienced was quite remarkable. After our second session one of the men shared his experience in hearing from God. He was commuting to work on the train, where he was spending time abiding in the Word. As he was talking to God, he asked a question about a business situation. **God answered** and gave him the solution. He could hardly contain himself when he came to the third session and shared his experience. He had heard God's voice, and realized that with no religious or biblical maturity, he could develop an intimate relationship with Him and have a heart to hear. Within one month, all heard God's voice regarding specific issues in their lives and were on fire to enjoy this privilege that is available to all of God's children.

THOUGHTS

The understanding that I need to have a conversation with God is not often taught, even though the scriptures are clear in that regard. Am I really talking *with* God or instead talking *at* Him? Am I providing time to listen? Do I clearly understand His voice or does there seem to be some interference?

Write down your thoughts on what can be done to improve your ability to listen, hear and follow God.

Living The Restored Life

CHAPTER 4

The Steps Of Abiding: Spending Time In the Written Word

How do we study the Bible? Professors, teachers, preachers and laity all take many different approaches. One of the reasons for this variety of techniques is the objective of the individual performing the study. Perhaps a better question would be, *why* do we study the Bible?

Most of us who recognize and accept the authority and veracity of the scriptures study them in order to gain insight and understanding into personal matters of relationship or behavior. We also study to gain insight into what is happening in the broader spectrum of human events.

Most of us want to gain knowledge from our study. We sense this knowledge will help us improve our lives. To some extent, this is true. We must have knowledge in order to address issues. Unfortunately, there is a tendency to reduce our time studying scripture once we have acquired this knowledge. In such cases, the benefit God provides through His written Word is minimized.

We previously learned that knowledge without application is useless. God desires we allow this knowledge to be transferred to understanding, application and action. The primary purpose of the scriptures is not just to inform, but to move us to experience the reality of what is written. It is the wisdom of God we should be seeking. Since He is wisdom, we desire Him to help us grasp what is being said and move it to specific application and activity in our lives.

In this chapter, we will learn how to make that happen. We will address our time in the Bible from the perspective of allowing the Father to transfer His wisdom to us. While there are many advantages to this approach, one of the key benefits is the excitement of pursuing what He is saying through His written Word. Our time in the Word is no longer reduced to "study" or "devotional" time, but becomes an active desire to seek and apply what the Father has to say.

IT IS ESSENTIAL TO "LIFE".

The Word is spirit and it is life, and the flesh counts for nothing. (John 6:63). Jesus says He is the Bread of Life and we are to "feed" on Him. As He also is the Word (logos), we are to consume His Word, which contains life and power to speak to us and bring real transformation in our lives.

It Is Inspired by God.

II TIMOTHY 3:14-16

> *You, however, continue in the things you have learned and become convinced of, knowing from whom you have learned them, and that from childhood you have known the sacred writings which are able to give you the wisdom that leads to salvation through faith which is in Christ Jesus. All Scripture is inspired by God and profitable for teaching, for reproof, for correction, for training in righteousness; so that the man of God may be adequate, equipped for every good work.*

The Steps Of Abiding: Spending Time In the Written Word

The living Word of God is the very breath of God. It is inspired by Him and provides wisdom necessary for His children to live fruitful and restored lives. It equips us to understand and accomplish every good work God has planned for us.

It Is Supernaturally Spoken.

II Peter 1:16-21

> *For we did not follow cleverly devised tales when we made known to you the power and coming of our Lord Jesus Christ, but we were eyewitnesses of His majesty. For when He received honor and glory from God the Father, such an utterance as this was made to Him, by the Majestic Glory, "This is My beloved Son with whom I am well-pleased"—and we ourselves heard this utterance made from heaven when we were with Him on the holy mountain. So we have the prophetic word made more sure, to which you do well to pay attention as to a lamp shining in a dark place, until the day dawns and the morning star arises in your hearts. But know this first of all, that no prophecy of Scripture is a matter of one's own interpretation, for no prophecy was ever made by an act of human will, but men moved by the Holy Spirit spoke from God.*

The Scriptures are inspired by the Holy Spirit and originated from God, not men. The Bible is not a philosophy book, a set of principles or a recipe for living. It is the very word of God, written with the intention to bring us life, in abundance.

It Is Eternal in Nature.

Deuteronomy 11:18-24

> *"You shall therefore impress these words of mine on your heart and on your soul; and you shall bind them as a sign on your hand, and they shall be as frontals on your forehead. You shall teach them to your sons, talking of them when you sit in your house and when you walk along the road and when you*

> *lie down and when you rise up. You shall write them on the doorposts of your house and on your gates, so that your days and the days of your sons may be multiplied on the land which the LORD swore to your fathers to give them, as long as the heavens remain above the earth. For if you are careful to keep all this commandment which I am commanding you to do, to love the LORD your God, to walk in all His ways and hold fast to Him, then the LORD will drive out all these nations from before you, and you will dispossess nations greater and mightier than you. Every place on which the sole of your foot treads shall be yours; your border will be from the wilderness to Lebanon, and from the river, the river Euphrates, as far as the western sea."*

God provided His written Word for us to receive and then live accordingly. He desires us to experience the privilege of being restored back to the "Garden of Life", where everything is exceptional and superabundant. It is not just a book to be read by pastors and Christian workers, or to be left on the shelf and heard only when we attend church. Rather, it is to be the essence of each believer's daily life.

It Provides Direction.

Psalm 119:105-108, 130-135

> *Your word is a lamp to my feet and a light to my path. I have sworn and I will confirm it, that I will keep Your righteous ordinances. I am exceedingly afflicted; revive me, O LORD, according to Your word. O accept the freewill offerings of my mouth, O LORD, and teach me Your ordinances. My life is continually in my hand, yet I do not forget Your law...*

> *The unfolding of Your words gives light; It gives understanding to the simple. I opened my mouth wide and panted, for I longed for Your commandments. Turn to me and be gracious to me, After Your manner with those who love Your name. Establish my footsteps in Your word, And do not let any iniquity have dominion over me. Redeem me from*

the oppression of man, that I may keep Your precepts. Make Your face shine upon Your servant, And teach me Your statutes.

Life is confusing, filled with many obstacles and opposing forces. God gives us the scriptures to bring clarity and understanding. They are not too mysterious or difficult for anyone to receive. He can interpret and communicate them. A person's understanding of the Word, as it applies to his life, is not dependent on intellectual or spiritual maturity. Rather it requires a heart to hear and a desire to walk in the truths of God.

It Contains Eternal Life.

JOHN 6:63, 68; 17:3

"It is the Spirit who gives life; the flesh profits nothing. The words that I speak to you are spirit, and they are life." Simon Peter answered Him, "Lord, to whom shall we go? You have words of eternal life…"

"This is eternal life, that they may know You, the only true God, and Jesus Christ whom You have sent.

God's words are not intended to just provide rules and laws for us to follow. They speak to the heart of our being and reveal eternal life. Christ defines this as experiencing Him and the Father. We are led into an intimate relationship with Christ. This is a loving, two-way, favored relationship that allows us to live the victorious, restored life.

MEDITATE ON ITS CONTENT.

God invites us to meditate on His Word, not just read and study its content. We are to spend time "camping out" in the Word, truly meditating on its content. We should stay in the presence of God long enough for the truth of the Word to sink into our hearts. We can then live and experience its promises and truth in our lives. Remember, we are not reading a book but meditating on the very life and person of our Lord Jesus Christ. Our desire is for the Word to help us become more like Him.

Understand Its Instruction.

JOSHUA 1:6-9

> "Be strong and courageous, for you shall give this people possession of the land which I swore to their fathers to give them. Only be strong and very courageous; be careful to do according to all the law which Moses My servant commanded you; do not turn from it to the right or to the left, so that you may have success wherever you go. This book of the law shall not depart from your mouth, but you shall meditate on it day and night, so that you may be careful to do according to all that is written in it; for then you will make your way prosperous, and then you will have success. Have I not commanded you? Be strong and courageous! Do not tremble or be dismayed, for the LORD your God is with you wherever you go."

As we approach our lives with the desire for victory, we need guidance and direction. Meditating on the written Word gives us clear instruction. As we meditate, we understand its message. We will desire more and be intent on following its instructions. This will lead to more success in our lives.

Seek Its Insight and Satisfaction.

PSALM 119:97-103

> O how I love Your law! It is my meditation all the day. Your commandments make me wiser than my enemies, for they are ever mine. I have more insight than all my teachers. For Your testimonies are my meditation. I understand more than the aged, because I have observed Your precepts. I have restrained my feet from every evil way, that I may keep Your word. I have not turned aside from Your ordinances, For You

The Steps Of Abiding: Spending Time In the Written Word

Yourself have taught me. How sweet are Your words to my taste! Yes, sweeter than honey o my mouth.

Our role is to pursue the Word passionately, with a desire for insight and understanding. Such pursuit will lead us to belief and discernment regarding decisions and activities. It will also help to avoid choices, which could have adverse consequences in our lives. As we meditate on the Word, we will find it to be more and more desirable and wonderful than anything else in life.

Gain Its Perspective

PSALM 1:1-3

How blessed is the man who does not walk in the counsel of the wicked, Nor stand in the path of sinners, Nor sit in the seat of scoffers! But his delight is in the law of the LORD, and in His law he meditates day and night. He will be like a tree firmly planted by streams of water, which yields its fruit in its season and its leaf does not wither; And in whatever he does, he prospers.

The Word of God is intended to be so delightful that we will passionately meditate on it, day and night. It doesn't necessarily mean we will have a Bible in front of us all day long. Instead, we will want to ponder and consider the truths God is speaking into our hearts. It will be so desirable that we will constantly want to receive more revelation. Our openness to the Word will become more vivid and clear.

ALLOW SCRIPTURE TO "SPEAK".

The Word is not just for intellectual study or the acquisition of information. It is to be received into our lives. Christ speaks His Word by taking Logos (the written Word) and speaking it as Rhema (the spoken Word) to us personally. This Word applies to our situations, activities and experiences. We allow Him to speak as we read, meditate, ponder and pray on its content.

It Speaks Life.

DEUTERONOMY 8:1-3

> *All the commandments that I am commanding you today you shall be careful to do, that you may live and multiply, and go in and possess the land which the LORD swore to give to your forefathers. You shall remember all the way which the LORD your God has led you in the wilderness these forty years, that He might humble you, testing you, to know what was in your heart, whether you would keep His commandments or not. He humbled you and let you be hungry, and fed you with manna which out of you did not know, nor did your fathers know, that He might make you understand that man does not live by bread alone, but man lives by everything that proceeds out of the mouth of the LORD.*

As we meditate on the Word, we allow it to speak about life. We realize His words are not law or rules but our daily food, nourishing and providing sustenance to our soul and spirit. The Word becomes the very center of our being.

It Speaks Value.

JOB 23:10-14

> *"But He knows the way I take; When He has tried me, I shall come forth as gold. My foot has held fast to His path; I have kept His way and not turned aside. I have not departed from the command of His lips; I have treasured the words of His mouth more than my necessary food. But He is unique and who can turn Him? And what His soul desires, that He does. For He performs what is appointed for me, and many such decrees are with Him.*

The Word is actually to be treasured, not rejected or ignored. It becomes so valuable that we continually abide every day, receiving all the Father has to say. It becomes pure pleasure and such a joy. It truly becomes a treasure.

It Is Pure and Untainted.

I PETER 2:1-5

> *Therefore, putting aside all malice and all deceit and hypocrisy and envy and all slander, like newborn babies, long for the pure milk of the word, so that by it you may grow in respect to salvation, if you have tasted the kindness of the Lord. And coming to Him as to a living stone which has been rejected by men, but is choice and precious in the sight of God, you also, as living stones, are being built up as a spiritual house for a holy priesthood, to offer up spiritual sacrifices acceptable to God through Jesus Christ*

As our lives are restored, we acquire a greater sense of assurance and truth. This is only possible through receiving and meditating on the Word of God. It is the source of our growth and maturity. It can be trusted for accuracy and reliability. We can construct our lives on its firm foundation.

It Speaks Direction.

PROVERBS 4:20-23

> *My son, give attention to my words; Incline your ear to my sayings. Do not let them depart from your sight; Keep them in the midst of your heart. For they are life to those who find them and health to all their body. Watch over your heart with all diligence, For from it flow the springs of life.*

The Word is of little value if it merely remains in the mind. It has to be processed until it sinks deeper into one's heart and soul.. It provides the very life that drives our being. If we inhibit its movement into our hearts, by definition we will remain in the world and self, outside the Kingdom of God. It is only when the Word penetrates our hearts that it provides the source of life necessary to restore direction and provide fullness of life.

It Speaks Wisdom.

COLOSSIANS 3:15-17

> *Let the peace of Christ rule in your hearts, to which indeed you were called in one body; and be thankful. Let the word of Christ richly dwell within you, with all wisdom teaching and admonishing one another with psalms and hymns and spiritual songs, singing with thankfulness in your hearts to God. Whatever you do, in word or deed, do all in the name of the Lord Jesus, giving thanks through Him to God the Father.*

As we meditate on the Word, it will remain in our minds. This is not a fleeting memory, something we experience for a moment and then lose. The Word will actually remain in our consciousness and in the recesses of our minds. It will transform our lives and give us confidence and strength. The more we meditate, the more it builds on our previous experiences. We grow and mature in godly understanding, wisdom and character.

INQUIRE WHEN NEEDING CLARIFICATION AND ANSWERS TO QUESTIONS.

Abiding in His Word should not be merely study. It is a dialogue with the Father. We often will not fully understand exactly what He is saying. We may initially feel confused about how it applies to our situation or how to respond to the promises He is speaking into our circumstances. God desires we ask questions, seek clarification and indicate our lack of understanding. He wants us to discern and clarify what He is speaking.

The Steps Of Abiding: Spending Time In the Written Word

To Keep Us Aligned With His Will

II Kings 22:13

Then Hilkiah the high priest said to Shaphan the scribe, "I have found the book of the law in the house of the LORD." And Hilkiah gave the book to Shaphan who read it. Shaphan the scribe came to the king and brought back word to the king and said, "Your servants have emptied out the money that was found in the house, and have delivered it into the hand of the workmen who have the oversight of the house of the LORD." Moreover, Shaphan the scribe told the king saying, "Hilkiah the priest has given me a book." And Shaphan read it in the presence of the king. When the king heard the words of the book of the law, he tore his clothes. Then the king commanded Hilkiah the priest, Ahikam the son of Shaphan, Achbor the son of Micaiah, Shaphan the scribe, and Asaiah the king's servant saying, "Go, inquire of the LORD for me and the people and all Judah concerning the words of this book that has been found, for great is the wrath of the LORD that burns against us, because our fathers have not listened to the words of this book, to do according to all that is written concerning us."

Psalm 119:33-40

Teach me, O LORD, the way of Your statutes, And I shall observe it to the end. Give me understanding, that I may observe Your law and keep it with all my heart. Make me walk in the path of Your commandments, For I delight in it. Incline my heart to Your testimonies and not to dishonest gain. Turn away my eyes from looking at vanity, and revive me in Your ways. Establish Your word to Your servant, As that which produces reverence for You. Turn away my reproach which I dread, for Your ordinances are good. Behold, I long for Your precepts; Revive me through Your righteousness

In order to stimulate our understanding, it is important to ask questions and seek clarity. God speaks in a grand and amazing way. Our worldly experiences tend to limit our comprehension. Because the Father desires an intimate relationship, He actually enjoys deeper conversations as we seek to gain better understanding. This happens as we question, clarify, seek more revelation and dialogue with the Father regarding His Word.

In a classroom, a good teacher encourages questions and open dialogue. This allows the teacher to communicate more clearly and improve the understanding of those asking questions. It is really not our role to intellectualize the Word. Instead, we are to receive communication from the Father. It is His role to communicate in ways we can understand. This is not done mechanically, but only as we are in relationship with Him.

To Receive Answers.

Jeremiah 6:16

> *Thus says the LORD, "Stand by the ways and see and ask for the ancient paths, Where the good way is, and walk in it; and you will find rest for your souls…"*

Matthew 7:7-8

> *"Ask, and it will be given to you; seek, and you will find; knock, and it will be opened to you. For everyone who asks receives, and he who seeks finds, and to him who knocks it will be opened."*

John 15:7-8

> *"If you abide in Me, and My words abide in you, ask whatever you wish, and it will be done for you. My Father is glorified by this, that you bear much fruit, and so prove to be My disciples."*

The Steps Of Abiding: Spending Time In the Written Word

JAMES 1:5-8

> ...But if any of you lacks wisdom, let him ask of God, who gives to all generously and without reproach, and it will be given to him. But he must ask in faith without any doubting, for the one who doubts is like the surf of the sea, driven and tossed by the wind. For that man ought not to expect that he will receive anything from the Lord, being a double-minded man, unstable in all his ways.

If we are truly in dialogue and intimate relationship with the Father, through His Word, we must allow Him the flexibility and time to respond. Again, this is not a "speed" study (racing through a devotional in the morning before going to work). We need to process the truth with back-and-forth dialogue, allowing Him to respond and give additional revelation and clarity. Inquiring allows the Father to give us answers to questions and issues in our lives. It removes boundaries to understanding and allows us to see without obstruction.

TRULY STAY "CAMPED OUT" IN THE WORD.

We constantly need to have the Lord release His Word to us. He provides confirmation and assurance that we have been transformed, received truth, are applying truth and are fully receiving His promises. Here are some guidelines to practice as we camp out in the Word of God:

1. Pursue your interest! What interesting word or thought from the Spirit has been piquing your interest? What do you already know that God has placed on your heart?

2. Write out the specific Scriptures! Get a good cross-reference study Bible with annotations and a concordance. The NKJV (*Spirit Filled Life Bible*) is particularly good as it includes translations of Greek and Hebrew words. The NASB, NEV, and Amplified

are also good translations. Try to avoid using a paraphrase as a primary Bible text, but use them only as additional help. Go to a good internet site for different translations. Spend some time understanding the context of the specific book of the Bible from which the verse is taken. Also, do not read just the specific verse, but read the entire paragraph for context.

3. Cross-reference specific verses by using a cross-reference study Bible, which will take you to other scriptures about that particular revelation. Perform individual word studies using the concordance at the back of your Bible or by using an internet site. As you spend time in cross-referenced or word study verses, let the "quickening" of the Spirit lead. Is this something He is speaking to you? If so, spend time further processing the passage. If not, do not spend further time but continue to cross-reference other verses or go to another verse from your word study.

4. Write down your thoughts:
   - What does this say about the character of God?
   - What has God done, what is He doing or what does He promise to do?
   - Are there any conditions to what God promises? (If…then)
   - What are my responsibilities or responses?

5. Go deeper into Hebrew and Greek meaning of the words He is speaking to you. There are some good internet sites where you can print the Hebrew or Greek word meanings. Or use a good concordance to find the derivative of key words.

6. Memorize the verses (word for word) that God has been speaking to you. Carry 3x5 index cards with you to assist in remembering and keeping these verses at the center of your consciousness.

7. Journal your thoughts!
   - Do I believe this in my heart (is it settled)? Why or why not? What do I struggle with? What experiences in my life appear contradictory to what I am receiving in the Word?
   - How do these words apply to my situation and me?
   - How is God calling me to adjust my life to Him and His will?
   - What thoughts come to me about all this?
   - Dialogue with the Father regarding your thoughts. Ask for clarity, understanding, wisdom and faith.
8. Pray the promises! Ask God to fulfill what He has said to you.
9. Commit time with an accountability partner, friend, or spouse, sharing your journal and what God is saying to you.
   - Discuss your feelings, reactions, and insights. Why are they important to you?
   - Study specific verses that each of you is sharing.
   - Pray these verses together as you meet with each other.
   - Make sure the partner also is meditating on the Word and listening to what God is saying.

MORE THAN WORDS

At our retreats, we ask each person to bring a Bible, since much of our time together is spent discovering God's truth through his written Word. In one particular retreat, none of the six couples brought Bibles. They stated that they did not know where they were in the house. They said they attended church, but never realized spending time in the written Word was important. They knew there was an Old and New Testament, but did not really know where to look for certain books and verses in the Scriptures. We fortunately had enough Bibles on hand for each person.

For one retreat, we increased our number of personal exercises by having each person write out certain Scriptures and describe what they meant to them personally. Each time the couples returned from their private exercises, they were overflowing with excitement. They realized the verses were inspirational and held truth that applied directly to their personal lives. By the end of the retreat, each heard God's voice and could not wait to spend more time in the Word. We gave them the Bibles and encouraged them to spend time every day abiding in the Word. We desired their weekend experience to provide greater excitement and fulfillment in their lives. Now they are teaching others to spend time in the Word. It truly transformed their lives and they are seeing amazing, supernatural works of God as they receive His truth and promises.

SUMMARY

It is important to remember the Bible is really God's spoken Word. Before it was written and compiled, it was spoken. So when we seek to gain its wisdom, insight and direction, it is important to let the words "speak" to us as well. They need to come off the pages of parchment into the depths of our hearts. As we invoke the various techniques outlined in this chapter, we want to allow the Father to speak what is being said to us directly.

Being a grandparent has many attached blessings. One is reading to younger grandchildren before bedtime. Most of the time they are intensely engaged in the book. Often there is a word or phrase they cannot understand, but they don't hesitate to ask questions and seek clarification of what was read. They really desire understanding. That is what the Father wants us to do as we read, study, contemplate and internalize His written Word. Let it come to life, *our life!*

The Steps Of Abiding: Spending Time In the Written Word

REFLECTIONS

As we understand the nature of true "Bible study", we see how our current methods fall short of the desired results. We also understand the need to approach the scriptures as God's spoken word as well. What is He saying to me as I read and contemplate the meaning? How does this apply to my life and/or to any issues and circumstances I am experiencing?

In the space provided, write your thoughts regarding how you intend to modify your current Bible study practices so the Father can more clearly and precisely speak to you. What value do you see in approaching the scriptures in this manner?

_____

_____

_____

_____

_____

_____

_____

_____

_____

Living The Restored Life

CHAPTER 5

The Steps Of Abiding: Prayer

Think of the person with whom you have your closest personal relationship. For many, it is their spouse. For others it is a family member, mentor, friend or colleague. One of the distinguishing characteristics of that relationship is the ability to communicate, be transparent and relate what is on one's mind without fear of reprisal or judgment. Usually, this relationship becomes closer and even more meaningful the more time is devoted to its continuity, quality and maintenance. Rarely do such relationships survive if there are long periods of absence, silence or lack of nourishment. While some may seek to be an "island unto themselves", it never works. Man was made for companionship through relationship. For Christians, the most essential and meaningful, long-lasting and beneficial relationship we can have is with the Father.

As we will study, prayer has many facets. It is essentially the way we communicate with the Father, in both its quantitative and qualitative components. It is an integral part of the abiding process. Many of the ingredients essential to a strong earthly relationship also apply to the way we relate to God. Frequency, honesty, two-way dialogue, acceptance, clarity and openness are required in our time with Him. Since this is our most important relationship, it is vital for us to move into a full and complete prayer life, allowing us to receive His insights, direction, understanding, power, promises, peace and all the other Kingdom resources He desires us to have and experience.

WHAT REALLY IS PRAYER?

To fully experience the Restored Life, it is important to communicate with the Father easily and clearly. This occurs through dialogue, discussion, listening, asking questions and receiving answers with clarity.

It Is Abiding.

JOHN 15:1-5

> *"I am the true vine, and My Father is the vinedresser. Every branch in Me that does not bear fruit, He takes away; and every branch that bears fruit, He prunes it so that it may bear more fruit. You are already clean because of the word which I have spoken to you. Abide in Me, and I in you. As the branch cannot bear fruit of itself unless it abides in the vine, so neither can you unless you abide in Me. **I** am the vine, you are the branches; he who abides in Me and I in him, he bears much fruit, for apart from Me you can do nothing.*

Prayer always begins and ends with a **relationship with Christ, abiding in the Vine.** It is not just giving our wish list to God. It emanates from an intimate relationship through our connection to the Vine (Christ). A prayer life has vitality and leads to deepening that relationship while nourishing our lives so they can be productive vehicles for God's activity.

It Is Entering God's Presence.

HEBREWS 10:19-22

> *Therefore, brethren, since we have confidence to enter the holy place by the blood of Jesus, by a new and living way which He inaugurated for us*

> *through the veil, that is, His flesh, and since we have a great priest over the house of God, let us draw near with a sincere heart in full assurance of faith, having our hearts sprinkled clean from an evil conscience and our bodies washed with pure water.*

As children of God, we have the privilege of direct access to God's throne room. There, we can have dialogue with the Father through Christ. God invites us to boldly enter His presence. We enter, not on the basis on our qualifications or level of spiritual maturity. It is based solely on the work of Jesus Christ as our High Priest. This is truly good news! Our entrance is not due to performance, rank or holiness. As His children, we all have free and equal access to God's throne room. Being part of the family, our access is not restricted. We are invited to come with authentic hearts. The Greek in this passage means to come with a real heart and express everything that is within us. We are not required to act in a ritualistic way. We have freedom to express our true feelings and thoughts with God.

It Is Depending on the Father

LUKE 11:1-13

> *It happened that while Jesus was praying in a certain place, after He had finished, one of His disciples said to Him, "Lord, teach us to pray just as John also taught his disciples." And He said to them, "When you pray, say: 'Father, hallowed be Your name. Your kingdom come. Give us each day our daily bread,* **and** *forgive us our sins, for we ourselves also forgive everyone who is indebted to us. And lead us not into temptation.' Then He said to them, "Suppose one of you has a friend, and goes to him at midnight and says to him, 'Friend, lend me three loaves; for a friend of mine has come to me from a journey, and I have nothing to set before him'; and from inside he answers and says, 'Do not bother me; the door has already been shut and my children and I are in bed; I cannot get up and give you anything.' I tell you, even though he will not get up and*

give him anything because he is his friend, yet because of his persistence he will get up and give him as much as he needs. So I say to you, ask, and it will be given to you; seek, and you will find; knock, and it will be opened to you. For everyone who asks, receives; and he who seeks, finds; and to him who knocks, it will be opened. Now suppose one of you fathers is asked by his son for a fish ; he will not give him a snake instead of a fish, will he? Or if he is asked for an egg, he will not give him a scorpion, will he? If you then, being evil, know how to give good gifts to your children, how much more will your heavenly Father give the Holy Spirit to those who ask Him?"

Our prayer life is intended to be a daily, ongoing relationship where we dialogue with the Father and are drawn into His bigger story. Prayer is not just repeating what is called the "Lord's Prayer". However, it should include those elements related to that prayer, such as:

- It addresses the Father
- It asks for the Kingdom to come (which means it doesn't appear automatically).
- It asks for His will to be done on Earth in the same way it is in Heaven (which also means it is not automatic, or we would not have to ask for it). Furthermore, God's will is perfectly carried out in Heaven. His instruction and the very power of Heaven are conveyed to us.
- It addresses daily issues, not dwelling on what has already happened, and means we are enjoying every day.
- It asks for His forgiveness and expresses that forgiveness toward others.
- It seeks His deliverance and protection. He brought us out of bondage and destructive patterns in order to live the Restored Life. We need to be protected from forces opposed

to His will. We must remain in the Kingdom and not be drawn to areas where we are unprotected and vulnerable.

- It persistently seeks His will until we have clarity. This will bring intimacy with Him and continue the dialogue until we fully understand what He promises to do. He wishes us to join Him in His directed activity.

- It asks, seeks and knocks. We ask Him to speak His will as we pursue information and understanding. This is part of our due diligence in looking for truth. We, then join Him without trying to make things happen on our own. We desire to know the goodness of the Father. He makes everything known and understood. Our prayers are answered according to God's will.

It Is Securing Wisdom.

JAMES 1:5-8

> *But if any of you lacks wisdom, let him ask of God, who gives to all generously and without reproach, and it will be given to him. But he must ask in faith without any doubting, for the one who doubts is like the surf of the sea, driven and tossed by the wind. For that man ought not to expect that he will receive anything from the Lord, being a double-minded man, unstable in all his ways.*

Since we lack wisdom about every decision (and particularly about things in the future), we are to ask the Father for insight and understanding. He promises to provide it liberally and with clarity so we fully understand His answers to our questions. It is conditional, though, because we must believe He will speak in a way we can hear and understand. Otherwise, He will not even bother speaking, since we would still be confused, unsure whether or not it is His answer we are hearing.

IT IS AN ACTIVE PROCESS (NOT REACTIVE)

II Samuel 7:25-29

> *"For You, O LORD of hosts, the God of Israel, have made a revelation to Your servant, saying, 'I will build you a house'; therefore Your servant has found courage to pray this prayer to You. Now, O Lord GOD, You are God, and Your words are truth, and You have promised this good thing to Your servant. Now therefore, may it please You to bless the house of Your servant, that it may continue forever before You. For You, O Lord GOD, have spoken; and with Your blessing may the house of Your servant be blessed forever."*

Our prayer life is intended to be very active. We tend to live passively, accepting everything as God's will. However, he desires we understand His specific will, including over seven thousand promises He wishes to convey and apply to our lives and situations. As we begin to understand that all the promises of God are "yes", we then ask the Father to speak these promises directly to us. We also desire clarity and ask Him to fulfill them. We have confidence He will do so, all of the time.

David understood three things from his intimate prayer life: the Father is God (and David was not), the Father's words were absolutely true, and these promises were spoken specifically to him. Upon reaching that understanding, he then prayed for God to fulfill what He promised. When Nehemiah was faced with the destruction of Jerusalem, he prayed and sought the Father's will for four months. The Father spoke a promise to him that had been given to Moses several hundred years before. God applied that Covenant promise to Nehemiah. He fully understood that this word and promise was intended for him and his situation. He believed and began to ask God to fulfill the promise, which He did. Thus prayer is also moving the promises of God into reality.

WHAT ARE THE HINDRANCES TO EFFECTIVE, BELIEVING PRAYER?

There are conditions in our lives that actually hinder God from hearing and answering our prayers. Though He loves and accepts us, He does require us to address and avoid these obstacles. He then can resume speaking to us, listening to us and fulfilling what He promises.

Iniquity in the heart

PROVERBS 15:29; 28:9-10

> *The heart of the righteous ponders how to answer, But the mouth of the wicked pours out evil things. The LORD is far from the wicked, but He hears the prayer of the righteous.*
>
> *He who turns away his ear from listening to the law, even his prayer is an abomination. He who leads the upright astray in an evil way will himself fall into his own pit, But the blameless will inherit good.*

PSALM 66:18

> *If I regard wickedness in my heart, The Lord will not hear.*

ISAIAH 59:1-2

> *Behold, the LORD'S hand is not so short that it cannot save; Nor is His ear so dull that it cannot hear. But your iniquities have made a separation between you and your God, and your sins have hidden His face from you so that He does not hear.*

Scripture clearly states we cannot assume that simply because we are children of God, our prayers are automatically heard and answered. If we cling to our own desires (by walking in self, not seeking the Lord and not desiring to walk in the Kingdom), our prayers are hindered and we are separated from the very power that desires to lead us into a fully restored life. Remember, the remedy is not to "fix" the iniquity but rather to confess, repent and return back into relationship with the Father.

Wrong Motives

JAMES 4:2-3

> *You do not have because you do not ask. You ask and do not receive, because you ask with wrong motives, so that you may spend it on your pleasures.*

When we possess the wrong motives, we ask for things we want God to do, rather than asking for God's will and His wishes. So many prayers are not answered because they are asked with the wrong intentions. We do not bring them to the Father with surrendered hearts. Wrong motives indicate we are not walking in the Kingdom, but rather in the flesh.

Doubt and Unbelief

JAMES 1:5-8

> *But if any of you lacks wisdom, let him ask of God, who gives to all generously and without reproach, and it will be given to him. But he must ask in faith without any doubting, for the one who doubts is like the surf of the sea, driven and tossed by the wind. For that man ought not to expect that he will receive anything from the Lord, being a double-minded man, unstable in all his ways.*

Even when we ask God for wisdom and insight, we can still hamper His willingness to communicate. This happens when we ask with skepticism and uncertainty. We often ask with a resignation He may not respond. He wants us to walk with Him and receive faith. Hebrews 12:1–2 says that He is the author and finisher of faith. However, when we ask in dialogue with Him, we must believe He will answer. If we do not believe, our prayers are hindered and our expectations limited. We must enter the conversation with the certainty He will respond.

Succumbing to Worldly and Selfish Desires
GALATIANS 5:16-21

> *But I say, walk by the Spirit, and you will not carry out the desire of the flesh. For the flesh sets its desire against the Spirit, and the Spirit against the flesh; for these are in opposition to one another, so that you may not do the things that you please. But if you are led by the Spirit you are not under the Law. Now the deeds of the flesh are evident, which are: immorality, impurity, sensuality, idolatry, sorcery, enmities, strife, jealousy, outbursts of anger, disputes, dissensions, factions, envying, drunkenness, carousing, and things like these, of which I forewarn you, just as I have forewarned you, that those who practice such things will not inherit the kingdom of God.*

Forces opposed to the Spirit of God can prevent us from walking in the Spirit and keep us out of the Kingdom. This directly hinders our prayers by keeping us away from the presence of God. Instead we occupy our minds and time with activities contrary to His will. We ignore time with Him and any communication we have is one-way at best.

Lack of Forgiveness
MARK 11:25-26

> *"Whenever you stand praying, forgive, if you have anything against anyone, so that your Father who is in heaven will also forgive you your transgressions. But if you do not forgive, neither will your Father who is in heaven forgive your transgressions."*

Lack of forgiveness is another indication we are not walking in the Kingdom. God's nature is forgiveness and if we were walking in the Kingdom with the Spirit, we would automatically have a forgiving heart. This gives us the power to forgive others, all of the time. Forgiveness is really not between two people, but between a person and God. Everyone can live in complete forgiveness, though they may lack reconciliation with some others. If we are not living in forgiveness, our prayers are being hampered. If this is the case, God tells us we have established a barrier to the dialogue.

Disobedience

HEBREWS 3:15-19

> *While it is said, "Today if you hear His voice, do not harden your hearts, as when they provoked Me." For who provoked Him when they had heart? Indeed, did not all those who came out of Egypt led by Moses? And with whom was He angry for forty years? Was it not with those who sinned, whose bodies fell in the wilderness? And to whom did He swear that they would not enter His rest, but to those who were disobedient? So we see that they were not able to enter because of unbelief.*

Disobedience is willfully doing the opposite of God's direction. We can still struggle with obedience as we continue to stay in dialogue with the Father and work through our issues. However, disobedience arises when we are resigned, just don't care and have decided our conclusions are better. It is difficult to communicate with the Father when we have chosen to live outside and perhaps directly opposite His desires for us.

Spiritual Attack

EPHESIANS 6:10-20

> *Finally, be strong in the Lord and in the strength of His might. Put on the full armor of God so that you will be able to stand firm against the schemes of the devil. For our struggle is not against flesh and blood, but against the rulers, against the powers, against the world forces of this darkness, against the spiritual forces of wickedness in the heavenly places. Therefore, take up the full*

armor of God, so that you will be able to resist in the evil day, and having done everything, to stand firm. Stand firm therefore, having girded your loins with truth, and having put on the breastplate of righteousness, and having shod your feet with the preparation of the gospel of peace; in addition to all, taking up the shield of faith with which you will be able to extinguish all the flaming arrows of the evil one. And take the helmet of salvation, and the sword of the Spirit, which is the word of God. With all prayer and petition pray at all times in the Spirit, and with this in view, be on the alert with all perseverance and petition for all the saints, and pray on my behalf, that utterance may be given to me in the opening of my mouth, to make known with boldness the mystery of the gospel, for which I am an ambassador in chains; that in proclaiming it I may speak boldly, as I ought to speak.

Daniel 10:10-15

Then behold a hand touched me and set me trembling on my hands and knees. He said to me, "O Daniel, man of high esteem, understand the words that I am about to tell you and stand upright, for I have now been sent to you." And when he had spoken this word to me, I stood up trembling. Then he said to me, "Do not be afraid, Daniel, for from the first day that you set your heart on understanding this and on humbling yourself before your God, your words were heard, and I have come in response to your words. But the prince of the kingdom of Persia was withstanding me for twenty-one days; then behold, Michael, one of the chief princes, came to help me, for I had been left there with the kings of Persia. "Now I have come to give you an understanding of what will happen to your people in the latter days, for the vision pertains to the days yet future." When he had spoken to me according to these words, I turned my face toward the ground and became speechless.

"Principalities and powers" are real, and they often hinder our prayers through true spiritual attacks. The enemy (forces seeking to keep us from the Father) fights against our dialogue with Him. These forces work to prevent answers from arriving and fulfilling God's purposes.

This is why it is so critical to put on the "armor of God" and fight this battle with spiritual weaponry, not worldly methods. As we properly "arm" ourselves, we are actually receiving the cover (protection) of the Father, Himself. Such attacks actually should cause us to move closer to God, where we know victory has already been won.

Lack of Unity with Spouse

1 Peter 3:7

> *You husbands in the same way, live with your wives in an understanding way, as with someone weaker, since she is a woman; and show her honor as a fellow heir of the grace of life, so that your prayers will not be hindered.*

Because God has called those in marriage to be one, when we are walking without unity, our prayers will be hindered. He desires both spouses enter into an intimate prayer life in the Kingdom of God with Him. There, they automatically will experience great unity together. If this does not occur, it indicates that one or both are outside of the Kingdom of God. Because God has called them to be one, their prayer life is hindered through this disunity. It is amazing how much stronger our prayer lives can be when we both actually seek the Father, especially when we pray together.

Cynicism, Resignation

James 4:1-2

> *What is the source of quarrels and conflicts among you? Is not the source your pleasures that wage war in your members? You lust and do not have; so you commit murder. You are envious and cannot obtain; so you fight and quarrel. You do not have because you do not ask.*

God says we lack things because we don't ask for them. When we resort to cynicism and resignation, we stop asking. We think prayer doesn't matter and therefore question why we should even bother. Actually, unanswered prayers should cause us to confess and repent. He wants us to return back into relationship and again experience His wonderful answers to prayer. If our lives are submerged in worldly or ungodly activity, we will not be in communication with the Father. If we lack confidence in His willingness or desire to answer, we resort to taking matters into our own hands. Failure to engage Him in conversation will not bring an answer.

WHAT ARE THE CONDITIONS TO ANSWERED PRAYER?

Answered prayers are not automatic. The Father desires we abide in Him and stay in intimacy with Him. Thus, our prayer life is not meant to be one-way communication where we give Him only our lists of wants and needs, day after day. Prayer is transparency and intimacy, back-and-forth dialogue. Through this intimacy, we understand the conditions under which the Father answers our prayers.

In His Name

JOHN 14:12-14

> *"Truly, truly, I say to you, he who believes in Me, the works that I do, he will do also; and greater works than these he will do; because I go to the Father. Whatever you ask in My name, that will I do, so that the Father may be glorified in the Son. If you ask Me anything in My name, I will do it."*

A condition to answered prayer is to pray in the name of Christ. Christ's name is "I Am", which means He is all and can be all things for us. As we pray in His name, we receive His authority and His promises and can speak them into a specific situation. This is not based on our resources or our abilities. It stands on the supremacy and sovereignty of God Almighty. Nothing is too difficult for Him. As we pray in His name under His authority, we recognize He is greater than our circumstances. We do not engage in wishful thinking, but confidently seek His will and authority over a particular situation.

His Words Abide in Us

JOHN 15:7-8

> *"If you abide in Me, and My words abide in you, ask whatever you wish, and it will be done for you. My Father is glorified by this, that you bear much fruit, and so prove to be My disciples."*

As we abide and dialogue with Him, He will speak Rhema words to us for our unique situations. As these words penetrate our hearts, we can believe and stand on their promises. We need to consider and remember what He has said. This allows us to be more focused on His will and our discussions to be more clearly understood.

Pray His Will

1 JOHN 5:14-15

> *This is the confidence, which we have before Him, that, if we ask anything according to His will, He hears us. And if we know that He hears us in whatever we ask, we know that we have the requests, which we have asked from Him.*

Another condition for answered prayer is to pray according to His will. He must first speak and clarify His will so we can then understand, pray, and expect to see it fulfilled. Often, we rush to action with a sense of resignation that whatever happens is God's will. This is not a walk of faith. He desires we seek Him first and are drawn into intimacy. We will hear His will and know what is on His heart and mind. Then we can move to activity.

The Steps Of Abiding: Prayer

Speak His Will with Boldness and Faith

MARK 11:20-24

> *As they were passing by in the morning, they saw the fig tree withered from the roots up. Being reminded, Peter said to Him, "Rabbi, look, the fig tree which You cursed has withered." And Jesus answered saying to them, "Have faith in God. Truly I say to you, whoever says to this mountain, 'Be taken up and cast into the sea,' and does not doubt in his heart, but believes that what he says is going to happen, it will be granted him. Therefore I say to you, all things for which you pray and ask, believe that you have received them, and they will be granted you."*

HEBREWS 10:19-25

> *Therefore, brethren, since we have confidence to enter the holy place by the blood of Jesus, by a new and living way which He inaugurated for us through the veil, that is, His flesh, and since we have a great priest over the house of God, let us draw near with a sincere heart in full assurance of faith, having our hearts sprinkled clean from an evil conscience and our bodies washed with pure water. Let us hold fast the confession of our hope without wavering, for He who promised is faithful; and let us consider how to stimulate one another to love and good deeds,*

Once we understand His will, we must speak it publicly and boldly. This is a representation of our faith and confidence regarding God's will. It means we have spent intimate time with Him, heard Him speak and have clarity about His words. We then proclaim them in faith before something actually happens. As we live this way, we will see many supernatural and miraculous things happen. We know God is involved and receive His righteousness, peace and joy in the process.

Tap into His Power

MATTHEW 9:18-26

> *Jesus got up and began to follow him, and so did His disciples. And a woman who had been suffering from a hemorrhage for twelve years, came up behind Him and touched the fringe of His cloak; for she was saying to herself, "If I only touch His garment, I will get well." But Jesus turning and seeing her said, "Daughter, take courage; your faith has made you well." At once the woman was made well. When Jesus came into the official's house, and saw the flute-players and the crowd in noisy disorder, He said, "Leave; for the girl has not died, but is asleep." And they began laughing at Him. But when the crowd had been sent out, He entered and took her by the hand, and the girl got up. This news spread throughout all that land.*

MALACHI 4:1-3

> *"For behold, the day is coming, burning like a furnace; and all the arrogant and every evildoer will be chaff; and the day that is coming will set them ablaze," says the LORD of hosts, "so that it will leave them neither root nor branch. But for you who fear My name, the sun of righteousness will rise with healing in its wings; and you will go forth and skip about like calves from the stall. You will tread down the wicked, for they will be ashes under the soles of your feet on the day which I am preparing," says the LORD of hosts.*

A woman with a physical problem decided to touch the helm of Christ's garment in order to heal her bodily affliction. She understood (as she surrendered her will to Christ by touching Him) His power was available to her. There are numerous places in the Old Testament where the term "healing in His wings" literally means healing in the hems of His garment. To tap into His power, we are to pray with a surrendered heart and recognize His power comes into our lives and our situations. We should expect the Father's results to be displayed, results that contain His supernatural touch. Any time the Father is engaged, the results are supernatural.

Unity

Psalm 133:1-3

> *Behold, how good and how pleasant it is for brothers to dwell together in unity! It is like the precious oil upon the head, Coming down upon the beard, Even Aaron's beard, coming down upon the edge of his robes. It is like the dew of Hermon coming down upon the mountains of Zion; for there the LORD commanded the blessing—life forever.*

Matthew 18:18-20

> *"Truly I say to you, whatever you bind on earth shall have been bound in heaven; and whatever you loose on earth shall have been loosed in heaven. Again I say to you, that if two of you agree on earth about anything that they may ask, it shall be done for them by My Father who is in heaven. For where two or three have gathered together in My name, I am there in their midst."*

The Father places a premium on unity. He commands blessing (which means it will happen) when we reach unity. Together as we understand, receive and proclaim His will, we can pray and expect Him to fulfill what He has spoken. Unity is not negotiation! It is coming together, in the Spirit, to see what's on the heart and mind of God. With that unified clarity, we are able to pray together for it to be fulfilled. Unity leads to a powerful response and engagement by the Father.

Examples of Prayers: These are numerous examples of believing prayers by those, who were not hindering God, but were hearing and responding, meeting the conditions for answered prayer. Read a few of these to see how these people of God prayed and how God answered their prayers.

1. Moses – Exodus 15:22-27

2. David – 1 Samuel 23:1-13

3. Solomon – 1 Kings 3:1-14

4. Hezekiah/Isaiah – II Kings 20:1-6

5. Abijah – II Chronicles 13:1-22

6. Jehoshaphat – II Chronicles 20:1-25

_____

_____

_____

7. Nehemiah – Nehemiah 1:1-11; 9:1-38

_____

_____

_____

8. Jeremiah – Jeremiah 15:10-21

_____

_____

_____

9. Daniel – Daniel 9:1-27

_____

_____

_____

10. Habakkuk – Habakkuk 1:1 – 2:4

_____

_____

_____

11. Jesus – John 11:38-44; 17:1-26

_____
_____
_____

12. Ananias – Acts 9:1-19

_____
_____
_____

13. Peter – Acts 9:32-43;10:9-43

_____
_____
_____

14. Paul

- Ephesians 1:15-23
- Ephesians 3:14-21
- Philippians 1:3-11
- Colosians 1: 9-18

_____
_____
_____
_____

"EVEN THE WINDS AND SEA OBEY HIM"
Matthew 8:27

It was the last day of our family vacation, an annual jaunt to the beach where the entire crew gathers in one house and shares food, rooms, convenience and inconvenience. We had been doing this for many years. It was a throwback to the many past vacations we had taken when our children were young. Now they had their own families and yet, were still excited and looking forward to this time together.

We had completed four days of our week-long stay when my wife, came down with a miserable case of summer flu. She was so ill she spent an entire day in bed. That was quite unlike her. In fact, she was always the healthiest member of the family so when she remained in her room, we knew she was not well.

The next day it rained throughout the day. We were unable to go to the beach, so we headed to the nearest town to pick up some staples and perhaps shop. As soon as we arrived, she was too sick to continue and we headed back to the house for more rest. She also spent the rest of that day in bed.

Day seven was our last day. I noticed the sun shining through the window and headed for the beach. She felt better and thought she could spend the day under an umbrella with other family members. I took the canopy and tediously raised the cover while anchoring the legs. No one saw me and I became rather perturbed by the lack of assistance in this effort.

When I finished, I noticed some people heading for their homes and folding up their umbrellas and chairs. I looked at the ocean and saw a huge storm front approaching the beach. I don't know how I missed it earlier, but was so absorbed in raising the canopy, I just didn't notice. My first reaction was to begin disassembling the canopy. Instead, I said to the Father, "This is our last day of vacation and my wife has not been able to enjoy her time here for the last two days. Would you please stop this storm and keep it away?"

Everyone seemed to be scurrying to safety. I heard that small internal voice reply, *"I am willing to do so! Now what will you do to show you believe Me"?* I was somewhat surprised by the response. I thought I could go back inside and watch Him do His work. That clearly would not have been the response He wanted. So, I went back to our house, grabbed a book, four folding chairs and returned to the beach.

I sat there and started to read the book, cautiously peeking over the pages to see the storm getting closer. It didn't look like it was going to recede or dissipate and I began to wonder if my "bold" move was appropriate. More and more people went back to their homes. I suddenly noticed a very small break begin in the center of the front as it approached the beach. It was small, but it provided a flicker of hope.

Suddenly the space grew quickly and the storm began to separate. One part headed west and the other continued toward the beach. The part heading west quickly went down the beach, ceasing to remain a threat to the area. However, the remaining part continued toward the beach and seemed to hover above our canopy. I noticed raindrops beginning to fall. At that point, I rose from the chair and left the protection of the cover. I looked up at the dark and dense clouds remaining and said, "Who do you think you are? The Father told you to go away; now get out of this place!" I had never been so bold before in asserting what the Father had told me. Immediately, as if responding to my internal call, the storm began to move and dissipated within five minutes.

The sun immediately returned and it was a beautiful day. We all had a great time together. Her strength returned and we were blessed with an wonderful ending to our family gathering. I was awed at the Father's willingness to respond in such a mighty way to what most people would consider a rather trivial item. But it was important to us and apparently to Him.

The Steps Of Abiding: Prayer

SUMMARY

Prayer is the way we communicate with the Father. It encompasses conversation, communication, clarification, and generally all aspects of the way we stay in touch with our Creator. That's why we are encouraged to pray in all matters, leaving nothing outside the Father's consideration. We are instructed to "ask, seek and knock". That occurs when we directly engage the Father in communication. A prayerful attitude is one in which we recognize we are talking to God, Himself. Our hearts fully realize we are conversing and communicating with the creator, sustainer and sovereign ruler of the universe. Does this not require an attitude of reverence and awe?

Through prayer we receive the Word and allow the Spirit of the Father to enter our reality here on Earth. When we pray, we enter the Kingdom, become "in Christ" and start the process of abiding. Let us not grow weary of engaging the Father, moment by moment and day by day.

CHAPTER 6

The Steps Of Abiding: Journaling

Do you remember taking notes during important classes in high school and/or college? Do you remember what happened when you didn't? We need a source of reference to help us retain information, making it available for use when facing a "test". Otherwise, it is usually "deleted" or "trashed", not available for a time when it could be useful or necessary.

What information is more important than words from the Father? We need to treat them with the care and completeness we would use for any other significant educational pursuit. When we pay close attention to what God speaks, we realize His words contain the most crucial and important information we can ever acquire. And, they come from the eternal giver and sustainer of life. This should cause us to document the conversation.

Journaling creates a record we can refer to for clarification and guidance. It brings together all aspects of abiding; personally hearing God's voice, receiving wisdom from the written Word and dialoguing with the Father through prayer. This allows us to retain our insights and further progress from what we have already learned. Let's pursue more insight into the reasons journaling is so important and the benefits we receive when we undertake this discipline.

REMEMBERING

PSALM 77:11-12

> *I shall remember the deeds of the LORD; Surely I will remember Your wonders of old. I will meditate on all Your work and muse on Your deeds.*

PSALM 143:1-5

> *I will extol You my God, O King, And I will bless Your name forever and ever. Every day I will bless You, and I will praise Your name forever and ever. Great is the LORD, and highly to be praised, And His greatness is unsearchable. One generation shall praise Your works to another, And shall declare Your mighty acts. On the glorious splendor of Your majesty and on Your wonderful works, I will meditate.*

Journaling consists of recording truth and pursuing God in our everyday lives. It helps us recall miracles, meditate and gain a better understanding of the Father's activity. When we chronicle the beauty and wonder of all He says and does, it provides encouragement. As we recall the wonderful direction and insight of God, we receive confidence and hope for issues and events we face today and in the future.

TEACHING

EXODUS 17:11-14

> *So it came about when Moses held his hand up, that Israel prevailed, and when he let his hand down, Amalek prevailed. But Moses' hands were heavy. Then they took a stone and put it under him, and he sat on it; and Aaron and Hur supported his hands, one on one side and one on the other. Thus his hands*

The Steps Of Abiding: Journaling

were steady until the sun set. So Joshua overwhelmed Amalek and his people with the edge of the sword. Then the LORD said to Moses, "Write this in a book as a memorial and recite it to Joshua, that I will utterly blot out the memory of Amalek from under heaven." Moses built an altar and named it The LORD is My Banner; and he said, "The LORD has sworn; the LORD will have war against Amalek from generation to generation."

EXODUS 24:1-4

Then He said to Moses, "Come up to the LORD, you and Aaron, Nadab and Abihu and seventy of the elders of Israel, and you shall worship at a distance. Moses alone, however, shall come near to the LORD, but they shall not come near, nor shall the people come up with him." Then Moses came and recounted to the people all the words of the LORD and all the ordinances; and all the people answered with one voice and said, "All the words which the LORD has spoken we will do!" Moses wrote down all the words of the LORD. Then he arose early in the morning, and built an altar at the foot of the mountain with twelve pillars for the twelve tribes of Israel. He sent young men of the sons of Israel, and they offered burnt offerings and sacrificed young bulls as peace offerings to the LORD.

EXODUS 34:24-28

"For I will drive out nations before you and enlarge your borders, and no man shall covet your land when you go up three times a year to appear before the LORD your God. You shall not offer the blood of My sacrifice with leavened bread, nor is the sacrifice of the Feast of the Passover to be left over until morning. You shall bring the very first of the first fruits of your soil into the house of the LORD your God. You shall not boil a young goat in its mother's milk." Then the LORD said to Moses, "Write down these words, for in accordance with these words I have made a covenant with you and with Israel." So he was there with the LORD forty days and forty nights; he did not

> eat bread or drink water. And he wrote on the tablets the words of the covenant, the Ten Commandments.

Journaling allows us to teach and pass on truth to others. It provides documentation and bears witness to the wonderful works of God in our lives, by recording what God has spoken. Because revelation is progressive (not all at once, but step-by-step and built upon previous statements) it is critical to write down each revelation we receive from the Father. Otherwise, we forget, regress and need to start over. Building on this progressive process of revelation is important to a deeper abiding relationship.

IDENTIFICATION

JEREMIAH 15:15(B) -16

> *Do not, in view of Your patience, take me away; Know that for Your sake I endure reproach. Your words were found and I ate them, And Your words became for me a joy and the delight of my heart; for I have been called by Your name, O LORD God of hosts.*

When we're recording our dialogue with the Father, our joy will greatly increase. It will deepen our relationship. It will solidify our understanding of our relationship to Him and encourage us to dwell on His very Word. This helps us to gain focus and avoid skipping those things He deems important and of high priority.

PRODUCTIVITY

JOHN 15:7-8

> *"If you abide in Me, and My words abide in you, ask whatever you wish, and it will be done for you. My Father is glorified by this, that you bear much fruit, and so prove to be My disciples."*

In order for us to be conscious of His words, we must spend time memorizing and processing what they say. Memorizing helps us to internalize His Word and apply it to our life situations and events. It also prevents us from neglecting or passing over significant revelation. It allows us to work more efficiently because we know His desires, they become ours and we utilize Kingdom resources instead of worldly ones. Our results become significantly better.

CONVERSATION

DEUTERONOMY 6:6-9

> *"These words, which I am commanding you today, shall be on your heart. You shall teach them diligently to your sons and shall talk of them when you sit in your house and when you walk by the way and when you lie down and when you rise up. You shall bind them as a sign on your hand and they shall be as frontals on your forehead. You shall write them on the doorposts of your house and on your gates."*

PROVERBS 7:1-4

> *My son, keep my words and treasure my commandments within you. Keep my commandments and live, and my teaching as the apple of your eye. Bind them on your fingers; Write them on the tablet of your heart. Say to wisdom, "You are my sister," And call understanding your intimate friend.*

As we record our dialogue with the Father, journaling becomes a forum for our conversations. We can share our writing with family, friends and children, so they gain the same understanding we have received from the Father. If your spouse and children are also journaling, this serves as a focus for open discussion and revelation. It serves to keep each other in prayer and intimacy with God. Furthermore, it will help us gain direction for our lives and remind us of our dependence on direction from God. He is the source and focus of our conversation.

We become more transparent in our relationships and our focus on truth becomes more intentional.

REMINDERS

I Corinthians 10:11,12

> *Now these things happened to them as an example, and they were written for our instruction, upon whom the ends of the ages have come. Therefore let him who thinks he stands take heed that he does not fall.*

Journaling helps to gain confidence in what we have heard. Reviewing and being reminded of what we have written leads and directs us to truth. It documents real-life examples that bear witness to truth. We experience a growing understanding of the nature, ways and purposes of God. It invites us to join His wonderful works. God wants to bless and keep us in His perfect will. Journaling keeps us aligned with His desires. This is so important because there are many external challenges to keep us from achieving this level of intimacy with Him.

HOW JOURNALING CAN CHANGE OUR BIBLE STUDY

Journaling tends to be the most difficult task to accomplish in the abiding process. We tend to think reading is sufficient. It does not take as much time as journaling. However, all of us can learn the beauty, necessity and value of journaling. I was discipling a CEO who was struggling with journaling. He was busy, not used to writing his thoughts and felt having the Bible on his computer was more efficient. I related how significant journaling would be to his intimate walk with God, and requested he practice journaling through an exercise. He should take a scripture that was meaningful to him, and write out the entire set of verses. He would write truths derived from these scriptures. The next step would be to write down what these verses were saying to him, personally. I asked him to fax me his journal pages. He faithfully completed steps one and two (to write out all the words of scripture verses and their truths).

When I read what the verses were speaking to him, there was a problem. It was written as if he was speaking publicly in church. It all sounded holy and righteous, but did not reflect any of his heart or his true responses to these truths. I related the journal was just between him and God (and me with permission). It was intended to be an authentic way of dialoguing with God about his understanding of God's truth. So I asked him to repeat step three and just write what was in his own heart. He should include any questions or items that were unclear or needed clarification from God.

The next time I read his faxed journal, it was quite different. I could see he was entering into a more intimate relationship with God by putting on paper what was in his heart. He also realized this and saw how meaningful journaling was to the process of abiding. He has continued since and has seen amazing revelation over time. Journaling takes truth from our head to our heart. It provides documentation we can review to avoid forgetting what God is saying to us.

SUMMARY

What do we do with the most important information we need? We usually record it in a place we know can be easily and quickly accessed. That's why our computers, notepads, and telephones are equipped with calendars, notes and stickers. That's why we create files to store e-mails, memos, documents or other material we may need to reference. It's also why we still keep papers and safekeeping material in file drawers and safety deposit boxes. While data storage has become increasingly digital in nature, the need for rapid retrieval has not abated. Who can remember all the IDs and passwords needed for numerous websites?

We need to treat the words and messages from the Father in the same regard. What could be more important to keep close and review often than the truth, wisdom, guidance and direction provided by Him? How easy it is to forget! So often we find ourselves mulling over issues, problems or other matters only to have the Father gently remind us He has already addressed them. When we take the time to journal and re-read what has been spoken, we are refreshed and renewed with an eternal perspective on our worldly matters. Journaling also creates a written connection of our lives with the Father's grand design. We receive written reminders of His enduring love and provision.

ACTION STEPS

Many of us schedule our activities, some on a daily basis. We want to ensure we have the time prepared to address the activity or issue at hand. We do this diligently, updating daily so we move forward with what seems an ever-increasing agenda of things to do. A few even prioritize before scheduling. They determine beforehand those items they need to address first, or what will require the most time for completion.

Whether this is recorded on some media or performed in our memory, why aren't we including God's direction in our time management? Why don't we treat His words as the highest priority and include any assignments from Him in our scheduling? Isn't this a way of clearing our path to ensure His will is done? Interestingly, when we do this, it is amazing how much more productive we become in the quality and quantity of our output.

In the space provided, write down the steps that can be taken in order to move God's agenda into our daily lives and consciousness. What can we do to increase the priority we assign to His work?

_____

_____

_____

The Steps Of Abiding: Journaling

CHAPTER 7

The Steps Of Abiding: Responding to the Father

The amount of data available in today's technologically driven society is growing exponentially. Having the most current and comprehensive information available is important but utilizing it is another matter. The desire and willingness to discern the correctness of available data, draw appropriate conclusions and then act accordingly is becoming a rare commodity. It is often difficult to grasp the validity, truth or usability of delivered communications. Often they are obscured by personal agenda, bias and deliberate misinformation. As a result, we are often paralyzed by inactivity, simply because we cannot trust the source or provider of the information.

We do not have this problem with the written or oral word of God. It can be clearly discerned and understood as we abide in Christ. Since it is His word, it can be trusted as truth. It can therefore move us to action without the limitations of the "blogosphere". Having said this, we still must act! When we do not, we limit the potential or intended results. In a biblical sense, this means the lack of activity to respond to God's message will render no "fruit". It actually results in weakening our connection to the Vine. We should desire the exact opposite.

As we journal our messages from God, we receive "life" from His Word. As we pray through and dialogue with the Father, recording all we are processing, God will challenge us to offer a surrendered heart in immediate and joyful obedience. As we respond to each directive, we will be able to move to the next step leading to an exceptional, restored life in the Kingdom. We live God's will, experiencing the best, the fullness of His being. We need to address this critical issue of obedience, discover its components and gain insight into any decisions we must make to allow the abiding process to move to completion.

SURRENDERING OUR WILL TO HIS AND PURSUING TRUTH WITH NEUTRALITY.

MATTHEW 16:21-27

> *From that time Jesus began to show His disciples that He must go to Jerusalem, and suffer many things from the elders and chief priests and scribes, and be killed, and be raised up on the third day. Peter took Him aside and began to rebuke Him, saying, "God forbid it, Lord! This shall never happen to You." But He turned and said to Peter, "Get behind Me, Satan! You are a stumbling block to Me; for you are not setting your mind on God's interests, but man's." Then Jesus said to His disciples, "If anyone wishes to come after Me, he must deny himself, and take up his cross and follow Me. For whoever wishes to save his life will lose it; but whoever loses his life for My sake will find it. For what will it profit a man if he gains the whole world and forfeits his soul? Or what will a man give in exchange for his soul? For the Son of Man is going to come in the glory of His Father with His angels, and will then repay every man according to his deeds."*

PSALM 86:11-17

> *Teach me Your way, O LORD ; I will walk in Your truth ; Unite my heart to fear Your name. I will give thanks to You, O Lord my God, with all my heart and will glorify Your name forever. For Your loving kindness toward me is great, And You have delivered my soul from the depths of Sheol. O God,*

> *arrogant men have risen up against me, and a band of violent men have sought my life, And they have not set You before them. But You, O Lord, are a God merciful and gracious, Slow to anger and abundant in loving kindness and truth. Turn to me, and be gracious to me; Oh grant Your strength to Your servant, And save the son of Your handmaid. Show me a sign for good, that those who hate me may see it and be ashamed, Because You, O LORD, have helped me and comforted me.*

To live a restored life, we must live in the Kingdom and walk in the Spirit with a surrendered heart. It is impossible to live in the Kingdom without a surrendered heart. Unless we subordinate our will to the Father's, we walk away from God. We miss the wonderful and fulfilling, restored life He has planned. We must have humility in our hearts with a desire and expectation for Him to lead and guide us into truth. But as adverse circumstances arise, we must daily, moment by moment, combat obstacles, remain focused on His will and follow Him. A surrendered will is a gateway into the Kingdom. We begin to recognize His will is best.

UNDERSTAND HIS INSTRUCTION AND GUIDANCE
Romans 8:12-17

> *So then, brethren, we are under obligation, not to the flesh, to live according to the flesh – for if you are living according to the flesh, you must die; but if by the Spirit you are putting to death the deeds of the body, you will live. For all who are being led by the Spirit of God, these are sons of God. For you have not received a spirit of slavery leading to fear again, but you have received a spirit of adoption as sons by which we cry out, "Abba! Father!" The Spirit Himself testifies with our spirit that we are children of God, and if children, heirs also, heirs of God and fellow heirs with Christ, if indeed we suffer with Him so that we may also be glorified with Him.*

Proverbs 3:1-6

My son, do not forget my teaching, But let your heart keep my commandments; For length of days and years of life And peace they will add to you. Do not let kindness and truth, leave you; Bind them around your neck, Write them on the tablet of your heart so you will find favor and good repute in the sight of God and man. Trust in the LORD with all your heart and do not lean on your own understanding. In all your ways acknowledge Him, and He will make your paths straight.

Proverbs 16:9

The mind of man plans his way, But the LORD directs his steps.

Our lives were intended to be in alignment with the Father. In order to live this life of relationship, it is vital we learn to hear and understand what He is saying personally and directly. God is not religious, nor is He distant. Our relationship is intimate. He speaks truth into our lives and we hear and respond with questions and dialogue. We reach clarity and understand what is on His heart. We should not move to action until we understand what He is saying. Obedience requires clarity. Otherwise, we bounce around seeking direction, often from the wrong sources.

RESPOND IMMEDIATELY.

John 14:19-24

"After a little while the world will no longer see Me, but you will see Me; because I live, you will live also. In that day you will know that I am in My Father, and you in Me, and I in you. He who has My commandments and keeps them is the one who loves Me; and he who loves Me will be loved by My Father, and I will love him and will disclose Myself to him." Judas (not Iscariot) said to Him, "Lord, what then has happened that You are going to

The Steps Of Abiding: Responding to the Father

> *disclose Yourself to us and not to the world?" Jesus answered and said to him, "If anyone loves Me, he will keep My word; and My Father will love him, and We will come to him and make Our abode with him. He who does not love Me does not keep My words; and the word which you hear is not Mine, but the Father's who sent Me."*

1 John 2:3-6

> *By this we know that we have come to know Him, if we keep His commandments. The one who says, "I have come to know Him," and does not keep His commandments, is a liar, and the truth is not in him; but whoever keeps His word, in him the love of God has truly been perfected. By this we know that we are in Him: the one who says he abides in Him ought himself to walk in the same manner as He walked.*

Living in the Kingdom and knowing His will provides the best in life. We need to be obedient to follow His instructions. We find it is a joy and pleasure to walk with Him, recognize His wonderful nature and all His beautiful plans. Disobedience, by definition, means we have decided to go our own way, thus exiting life in the Kingdom. Obedience is much greater than adherence to rules and regulations. It is responding to the direction and instruction He is personally giving, with the power to carry it out.

CONSTANTLY ABIDE AND SEEK CLARITY FOR CONFIRMATION AND SUPPORT OF OUR ACTIVITIES.

Deuteronomy 6:6-9

> *"These words, which I am commanding you today, shall be on your heart. You shall teach them diligently to your sons and shall talk of them when you sit in your house and when you walk by the way and when you lie down and when you rise up. You shall bind them as a sign on your hand and they shall be as*

frontals on your forehead. You shall write them on the doorposts of your house and on your gates."

Proverbs 7:1-4

My son, keep my words and treasure my commandments within you. Keep my commandments and live, and my teaching as the apple of your eye. Bind them on your fingers; Write them on the tablet of your heart. Say to wisdom, "You are my sister," And call understanding your intimate friend.

Exodus 34:27-28

Then the LORD said to Moses, "Write down these words, for in accordance with these words I have made a covenant with you and with Israel." So he was there with the LORD forty days and forty nights; he did not eat bread or drink water. And he wrote on the tablets the words of the covenant, the Ten Commandments.

As we remain in relationship, it is critical to remember the words He is speaking. Our understanding of those words, questions and thoughts become markers of the way God demonstrates His nature and revelations. We need to be constantly processing what the Father is saying. We should keep a record and refer to Him in all issues, circumstances or obstacles requiring further truth, insight and direction.

ALLOW GOD-DIRECTED ACTIVITY TO BE THE FOCUS OF OUR DAILY AGENDA.

We need to learn to let the Father's direction rise to the highest priority of our focus. In this way we remain in the center of His will. Our obedience must come from a continuous surrender each day. We must desire to commune constantly with the Father and receive His input and direction.

The Steps Of Abiding: Responding to the Father

Psalm 16:11

You will make known to me the path of life; In Your presence is fullness of joy; In Your right hand, there are pleasures forever.

Psalm 1:1-3

How blessed is the man who does not walk in the counsel of the wicked, nor stand in the path of sinners, nor sit in the seat of scoffers! But his delight is in the law of the LORD, and in His law he meditates day and night. He will be like a tree firmly planted by streams of water, which yields its fruit in its season And its leaf does not wither; And in whatever he does, he prospers.

Ephesians 2:10

For we are His workmanship, created in Christ Jesus for good works, which God prepared beforehand so that we would walk in them.

Because we are children of God, it is essential to schedule daily time when we can experience His presence. Here, we process His word and grow in our understanding of Him. We discover His supernatural power and witness its impact in our personal life. We learn He already has planned specific activity for our life. We find great joy and delight in His presence. We receive light, direction, guidance, transformation, fruits of the Spirit and His very nature. He needs to be the center of our lives, every day. He is life!

SUMMARY

In the book of James, we receive some very sobering advice, "But be doers of the word and not hearers only, deceiving yourselves...but a doer who acts, he will be blessed in his doing" (1:22,25b). This reminder is so critical to our abiding experience. Staying in touch with the Father is necessary, and actively following through on His input is absolutely required for us to receive the blessings and benefits He has in store.

If we receive an assignment at work, how do we respond? Chances are, if we want to keep our jobs, we will pay close attention to the details of the assignment and work diligently to ensure its execution in the specified time frame. We also remain aware of our responsibilities and duties, as outlined in our job description, in order to focus on those areas designated as our priorities. Why shouldn't our attitude be the same with the Father? Our desire should be to do the work He has provided (John 9:4). Should we not approach His directives in a manner that not only reflects the importance of the assignment, but also the position of the One providing the task? Where does the greatest benefit lie? What provides the best return on our investment of time and resources?

Once we grasp the realities of the Kingdom and an abiding relationship with the Father, our priorities will shift and the nature of our lives will change drastically. We must, however, remain desirous and intentional in working together with Him. To delay, procrastinate or even ignore what He asks is to forfeit the associated results, blessings and desires attached to the effort. That means we miss the "life" experience He desires and intends. Let us "not grow weary of doing good, for in due season, we will reap if we do not give up" (Galatians 6:4).

FOOD FOR THOUGHT

Surrender is a concept that runs contrary to our human nature. We interpret it to mean defeat, total loss and complete capitulation to our enemy. Therefore, it is to be avoided completely. The humiliation and costs associated with surrender are both detestable and undesirable.

From a biblical perspective, however, surrender has a much different meaning. God is not out to defeat or overpower us, but desires to bless, in abundance. When He asks us to surrender, He wants us to yield our wills, and desires in order to move to experience the fullness and completeness of the life He provides. In essence, He asks us to abandon our agenda in order to receive a more beneficial and enjoyable one. That is really the substance of our "cross". It is the will of the Father for our lives and He asks us to accept His alternative.

In the investment process, an investor transfers an amount of wealth into an asset with the hope of receiving a much higher return and value. We do the same when we "invest" in God's plan and transfer our life's goals and objectives to Him. Amazingly we discover, not only a greater return, but over time, our desires become more and more unified with His. Therefore, surrendering our lives to Christ is something we should desire and pursue. It is a key part of living the Kingdom life to a much greater degree.

How willing are we to surrender to Christ and His ongoing work in our lives? Are we open and desirous to fully surrender to His plan or to keep pursuing our own interests and destinies? In what ways do we need to change our focus and allow the Father to be the driver and sustainer of our time here on earth? What are your thoughts on this matter?

_____

_____

_____

_____

_____

_____

_____

SHERMAN'S MARCH

Sherman Strong is a pastor of a church located in St. Louis County, Missouri. Sherman entered the pastorate later than most, after a successful career with General Motors. But his road has not been easily traveled and, certainly, not without challenge.

After making a decision to enter the pastorate, Sherman was diagnosed with Stage IV liver cancer. At that time, and even now, that diagnosis was deemed terminal. Thus began the process of watching his weight fall and his body deteriorate. He began to experience other symptoms characteristic of the pathology associated with the disease. He became so weak he could no longer stand and had to be relegated to a wheelchair. If he desired to speak in church, he had to be raised by other members in order to be heard. The end appeared very close.

One Sunday morning, even though he felt terrible and had no desire to get out of bed, Sherman clearly heard God's voice telling him he would get through this. It sounded rather unbelievable given his condition, yet he also was convicted to tell the congregation. So, with the help of family members and friends, he was taken to church, wheeled to the front and raised to his feet. Although his voice was weak and barely audible, he told them God revealed he was going to be healed. One can only imagine the response of the congregation. The message from Sherman was just the opposite of the figure they witnessed before them.

Afterwards, Sherman noticed a change in the way he was feeling, even though his body did not appear to be changing. He did appear to be gaining some strength and his appetite for food began to return. One day during a visit to his doctor, he was observed to have a strange, unusual symptom that was not present earlier. The treatment was unorthodox and resulted in an outcome neither

Sherman, or the doctor expected. This occurred right in the office. Almost immediately, Sherman began to feel a reversal of all the symptoms associated with the disease. Over time, he returned to full health and began to see growth and other miraculous activity within the church.

God has now provided Sherman and his wife, Betty, a ministry that exceeds anything they had imagined. They continue to face the problems of a fallen world, but do so with confidence and faith in the Father. Sherman has also become a valuable counselor and advisor to many who have faced similar situations, including one of the writers of this book. While the medical community is unable to explain Sherman's outcome, he knows the source and the Healer.

CHAPTER 8

Conclusion

We have now finished this book. Is the living of a restored life now more desirable? Do we better comprehend the steps of abiding? More importantly, do we have a passion and desire to live this life, through Christ?

The Bible clearly points to a different life available for believers in Christ. Will we now move to take hold of that life and its promises and blessings? Or will we stay on our own path, content with our own agendas, efforts and the rewards they have provided? Will we remain satisfied with a "less than abundant" life? That's the challenge that lies before us. Here are some suggestions to help us advance faster in living the restored life.

ENJOY THE PRESENCE OF THE FATHER

How do we feel about being with the Father? Do we have joy and anticipation? Do we join Him with excitement and expectation? Do we feel at home and at peace when we are with Him? If not, it's probably because we haven't spent enough consistent time with Him or cultivated His presence. We want this relationship to reach the point where we begin to really know, enjoy, recognize and appreciate what a fantastic friend we have. For this to occur, we need to move from a ritual of prayer to transparent communication with the Father. This will lead to a life experience that surpasses any other relationship we possess.

GET IT SETTLED

In order to move to a Kingdom existence, we really need to get it "settled". This means we need to accept what scripture says as truth and reality. We can then move it to the level of experiential reality. Until then, Scripture will remain in the inventory of our minds as theological understanding or religious knowledge. It will not be magnified or witnessed in our daily living.

MAKE A DECISION

We must decide to seek the Father and begin to experience His supernatural love and power in all our relationships and activities. This must be a conscious, intentional decision on our part. No one can make it for us. It is ours alone! But we need to exercise our freedom and ability to make that choice and move ahead. No amount of procrastination or indecision will be of assistance.

RUN THE RACE

> ......"*But one thing I do, forgetting what lies behind and straining forward to what lies ahead, I press on toward the goal for the prize of the upward call of God in Christ Jesus. Let those of us who are mature think this way*" (Philippians 3:13-15).

We certainly enjoy winning. Whether it is our favorite sports team, college, high school, entertainment or other competitive event, we are always excited when first place is achieved. We enjoy being victorious. So should we also seek victory in the greatest race we will run; the quality and success of our lives. Will we succeed to the attainment of the "fullness of His glory", the abundance of life and fulfillment of His promises to us in this time we have on earth, or not? In this context, we certainly want to win. Therefore, we need to be prepared to:

1. Know the Competition

Even though there are many contestants, the battle to win is not against our earthly brethren. Instead Paul tells us it is against the "rulers, the authorities, the powers of this dark world and against the spiritual forces of evil in the heavenly places" (Ephesians 6:12). We therefore, need to recognize the race is spiritual. It is also against our selves. In Romans 7:23, we are reminded our mind and bodies are under attack to keep us disconnected from all the Father wants us to possess. While some of this is due to external forces, much is due to our own selfish objectives (James 1:14).

2. Don't Look Backwards

As the Philippians passage (above) reminds us, we do not ponder the past. Our focus is on what lies ahead. Therefore, we should not allow the constraints of our past actions and behavior to inhibit the future the Father has provided. We are always moving forward, just like eternity. Eternity never moves in reverse. It always advances. Through confession and repentance, the Father will allow us to deal with the consequences of the past. But He is always asking us to get on board and join Him in this exciting eternal journey.

3. Get in Shape

This is a long distance race, not a sprint. No victory is ever achieved in the first period. This race requires endurance and perseverance. We need to be in good condition. In Ephesians 6, we are told to put on the "whole armor of God" in order to stay in the race and win. We have been supplied with the "weaponry" we need to win. We do need to "put it on", i.e. integrate God's truth, righteousness, readiness, salvation and word into the heart of our very being. He also reminds us we should be self-controlled, purposeful, focused and disciplined as we live each day. Our advantages are many, but we need to be in a position to utilize them.

4. Walk First

We can't run this race until we first learn to walk. It is similar to the process of our physical growth and maturation. As we learn to "walk with Christ", we learn to utilize the resources the Father has provided. "To the healthy, walking is a pleasure, to the sick it is a burden, if not an impossibility. The walk to which He restores and empowers is like that of Enoch and Noah....a life like Abraham's ......a life of which David sings.....and Isaiah prophecies. This is the walk Jesus came to make possible to His people in greater power than ever before". (Murray, Andrew, "the Ministry of Intercessory Prayer").

Therefore, we need the practice the discipline of a good walk with Christ (learn to abide). Once this is attained, our speed can increase. On many occasions, Jesus would look at someone whose life He was miraculously changing and say, "Get up and walk". So we also should move out and begin walking this new life Christ has provided.

5. Understand what it Means to Win

Our comprehension of "winning" is usually conveyed in earthly terms and experiences. This normally means, "coming in first". It is the gold medal, the victory trophy or ring. It is landing the first place prize. Winning in life has a different connotation. Christ says that winning was "completing the work the Father gave Him to do" (John 17:4). That work "testified to who He was" (John 5:36). In John 9:4, He again emphasizes the importance of "doing the work of Him who sent me".

Paul seems to feel the same way. In Acts 20:24, he links "finishing the race" with "completing the task the Lord Jesus has given me". He compares the "working out of our salvation" in Philippians 2:12 with "acting according to His good purpose". In Ephesians 9:12, he links the "preparation of God's people for works of service" with "attaining to the whole measure of the fullness of Christ". And, finally in II Timothy 4:7,8, he states he has "finished the race, he has kept the faith" and remarks that he is ready for his "crown". So, for us, the race is to attain the maturity of knowing and reflecting Christ in our lives (becoming His image), by completing the work He has given us to do. This is our measure of victory.

6. Anticipate Victory

Our mindset should be one of a victorious people. While we should expect trials and trouble during our race (John 16:33), we must further realize Christ has already overcome them and "in Him", we have overcome the world (John 5:4). In Exodus14: 14, Moses instructs the Israelites, "the Lord will fight for you, you need only be still". It is important for us to remember this race is not to win on our ability, but it is Christ's to win for us. We run it through Him and with Him. If we stay in an abiding relationship with the Father, constantly aligning our lives with His word and will, then we should always expect to win. We should live and celebrate as victorious people.

Our deepest and most sincere prayers are for you and those close to you to experience the exceptional life that comes through knowing Christ. We trust this study will be of assistance in receiving this life. "In Him was life and that life was the light of men" (John 1:4). "He who has the son has life; he who does not have the Son of God, does not have life" (I John 5:12).

About the Authors

Larry Collett was an employee of Cass Information Systems from 1963 until his retirement in July 2008. He is currently the Chairman of the Board. He was hired by the company's banking subsidiary, Cass Commercial Bank, and held numerous positions culminating in his appointment as Executive Vice President in 1974. In 1990, he was elected Chief Executive Officer of Cass Information Systems, Inc. and was given the additional responsibilities of Board Chairman in 1992.

In 2007, Mr. Collett was named one of the nations best CEOs by DeMarche Associates, Inc., a Kansas City-based consulting company. Cass was also named by *Forbes* magazine as one of the nation's top 200 small public companies in 2006 and 2008. Cass is also a member of the Russell 2000, a well-recognized list of public companies selected for inclusion in this highly respected investment fund.

Larry's leadership combines two aspects of his life: a passion for new technology and a deeply held faith. His drive to incorporate newer technologies and his insistence on trusting God have been key ingredients of his business career.

In addition to his business responsibilities, Mr. Collett has held numerous positions with civic, charitable and church-related institutions. He was the Chairman of the Greater St. Louis Billy Graham Crusade in 1999. He also worked with several organizations that bring churches and pastors together in the St. Louis region. Larry chaired numerous fundraising activities for non-profit and educational institutions. He is a member of the Board of Regents of Trinity International University and Seminary in Deerfield, Illinois.

He has been a teacher of several courses for business, church and non-profit institutions. He is a member of the CEO Forum, an organization of Christian CEOs, and is on the adjunct teaching staff for the Spiritual Leadership Institute (SLI) of that organization. He has authored several

Bible studies, primarily related to the topics of "Abiding in Christ" and "Kingdom Restoration."

He attended St. Louis University, where he obtained both undergraduate and graduate degrees. He also performed post-graduate work at Rutgers University through the Stonier School of Banking. In 2014 he received the "Outstanding Alumni Award" from St. Louis University's Graduate School of Business.

A lifelong resident of the St. Louis area, Mr. Collett has been married to his wife Sharon since 1965. They have three children and nine grandchildren.

Richard T. Case, age 65, has over 45 years of executive line management experience, both as a senior executive with Fortune 500 companies and as a management consultant to numerous industries and companies. He has also been a featured speaker at numerous conferences and seminars. Mr. Case has received *The Wall Street Journal* Achievement Award, and is listed in *Who's Who in American Business*. Mr. Case holds an MBA degree from the University of Southern California where he graduated with a 4.0 GPA, first in the class; and a BS degree in Management and Finance from Bradley University, *magna cum laude*. He also graduated with a seminary Masters degree from Trinity Evangelical Divinity School, *summa cum laude*.

He and his wife, Linda, have started several new churches that remain strong today, and have served as interim pastors of troubled churches, bringing reconciliation and new vision to these situations. Currently, he and Linda are leading a fruitful, Christian marriage retreat ministry, "All for Jesus Living Waters Retreat Ministry". In addition to the retreats they personally lead, they now have over 16 couples trained as leaders who are conducting marriage retreats in their respective geographies around the country. Mr. Case is a published author, has hosted a weekly business radio program, and has served as a strategic consultant

About the Authors

to numerous non-profit organizations, including CEO Forum, Focus on the Family, and Navigators.

Richard lives in Castle Rock, Colorado, with his wife of 45 years. They both enjoy their five grandchildren and three grown children.

Authors' Note

Richard and Larry were given an assignment by the Father many years ago to receive understanding and revelation from the Word and communion with the Spirit about the Kingdom of God and the beauty of a "restored life." They then collaborated on two books to offer fellow believers what they have received. Understanding the Kingdom of God is critical to a believer's fulfillment of God's intended life for us. Through their understanding, living out these principles and now teaching them to others, they have established a reputation for helping others to live out a restored life in the Kingdom.

Additional Notes

The Restored Life

The Restored Life

www.ingramcontent.com/pod-product-compliance
Lightning Source LLC
Chambersburg PA
CBHW021153080526
44588CB00008B/314